Jessie. Day

Hymnal, for Christian Science Church and Sunday School Services

Jessie. Day

Hymnal, for Christian Science Church and Sunday School Services

ISBN/EAN: 9783337089856

Printed in Europe, USA, Canada, Australia, Japan

Cover: Foto ©Thomas Meinert / pixelio.de

More available books at **www.hansebooks.com**

FOR

CHRISTIAN SCIENCE CHURCH

AND

Sunday School Services.

Compiled and Arranged by

JESSIE DAY,

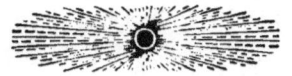

CHICAGO, ILL.:
MRS. O. W. DAY, PUBLISHER,
130 DEARBORN STREET.

Copyrighted by O. W. Day, 1889.

INDEX OF TUNES.

	PAGE
Alabaster	S. M. 175
Alida	C. M. D. 28
Aletta	7 27
Almsgiving	8, 8, 8, 4 18
America	6, 4 167
Amsterdam	7, 6, 7 44
Angels' Call	S. M. 111
Angels' Song	11, 10 137
Antioch	C. M. 62
Arcadia	C. M. 159
Arlington	C. M. 35
Armenia	C. M. 22
Athol	S. M. 114
Austria	8, 7, D. 180
Autumn	8, 7, D. 55
Avon	C. M. 12
Baden	S. M. 199
Baden	L. M. 141
Beatitude	C. M. 60
Beethoven	L. M. 52
Bemerton	C. M. 91
Benjamin	S. M. 160
Bera	L. M. 108
Berlin	10 86
Bethlehem	8, 6 86
Blumenthal	7, D. 165
Boardman	C. M. 133
Bonar	P. M. 204
Boylston	S. M. 154
Brattle Street	C. M. D. 117
Browne	6, 8, 4 39
Caledonia	7, 7, 7, 6 151
Carol	C. M. D. 68
Cheshire	C. M. 188
Christ Church	H. M. 63
Christmas	C. M. 16
Christmas Eve	H. M. 67
Christus Consolator	8.5,8.3 177
Chrysolite	L. M. 172
Clifford	C. M. 11
Clinton	C. M. 184
Come, ye Discousolate	11, 10 192
Cooling	C. M. 150
Cowper	C. M. 92
Creation	L. M. D. 42
David	8 21
Dedham	C. M. 20
Dennis	S. M. 149
Dover	S. M. 40
Downs	C. M. 57
Dulcetta	8, 7 185
Dwight	L. M. 115
Easton	L. M. 140
Eddy	P. M. 71
Elen	7 104
Ellacombe	7, 6 187
Elmswood	S. M. D. 153
Ernan	L. M. 14
Evan	C. M. 96
Evening Hymn	L. M. 51
Eventide	0 112
Ewing	7, 6 95
Faithful Shepherd	6 5 167
Father Most Holy	P. M. 45
Federal Street	L. M. 53
Fiat Lux	P. M. 4
Firth	P. M. 78
Foster	8 174
Geer	C. M. 54

	PAGE
Geneva	C. M. 157
Gennesaret	11 32
Germany	L. M. 143
Gloria Patri	205
God is Love	7 166
Gottschalk	7 56
Gould	C. M. 136
Gratitude	L. M. 126
Greenwood	S. M. 83
Hanover	11, 10 135
Haydn	S. M. 59
He Leadeth Me	L. M. 176
Hendon	7 191
Henley	11, 10 156
Herald Angels	7, D. 103
Hermann	C. M. 65
Hersal	C. M. 163
Holley	7 82
Holy Cross	C. M. 124
Home, Sweet Home	11 147
Hopkins	9, 8 8
Hummel	C. M. 48
Hursley	L. M. 179
Hyacinth	7 88
Ingham	L. M. 33
Innocents	7 98
In the Silent Midnight	8, 5 94
Italy	8, 4 100
Janes	L. M. 161
Jesus Shall Reign	L. M. 46
Jeshurun	7, 6, 7 61
Jewett	6 183
Keble	L. M. 74
Kelley	8, 7 197
Lebanon	S M. D. 102
Linwood	L. M. 84
Linwood	L. M. 90
Louvan	L. M. 50
Love Divine	8, 7, D. 93
Lowry	L. M. 79
Lux Benigna	10, 4, 10 31
Lyons	10, 11 9
Manoah	C. M. 139
Mara	C. M. 24
Marrion	P. M. 127
Mendelssohn	C. P. M. 5
Mendon	L. M. 119
Milwaukee	8, 7 171
Missionary Chant	L. M 160
Morning Star	7 130
Nauford	8, 8, 8, 4 162
Nearer to Thee	6, 4 10
Night Thoughts	L. M. 89
Northampton	L. M. 47
Nuremburg	7 152
Old Hundred	L. M. 205
Olivet	6. 4 196
Olmutz	S. M. 109
Ontario	L. M. 80
Orient	11, 10 200
Park Street	L. M. 73
Paulina	11 23
Pearsall	7, 6. D. 132
Percy	L. M. 30
Peterborough	C. M. 181
Pilgrim	8. 7 145
Pleyel's Hymn	7 85
Portuguese Hymn	11 37
Portuguese Hymn	11 201

	PAGE
Qui Habitat	Chant 206
Rathbun	8, 7 131
Redemptor Mundi	10 195
Redhead	8, 7, 8, 7 138
Refuge	7, D. 58
Requiem	8 7, 8, 7, 7 118
Rest	11, 10 34
Resurrection	10, 11, 12 77
Retreat	L. M. 170
Rilda	L. M. 19
Rischoline	8, 8, 8, 4 49
Rivaulx	L. M. 198
Rousseau	L. M. 113
Russian Hymn	10 194
Salome	C. M. 205
Salzburgh	7, D. 75
Savior, Like a Shepherd	8.7.4 41
Selvin	S. M. 7
Semper Aspectemus	C. M. 64
Serenity	C. M. 97
Seymour	7 36
Solitude	7 13
Somerville	L. M. 180
State Street	S. M. 134
St. Agatha	8, 7 69
St. Aelred	8, 8, 8, 3 158
St. Cecilia	L. M. 129
St. Hilda	7, 6 76
St. Matthew	C. M. D. 123
St. Nicolas	7. 5. 7, 5 105
St. Oswald	8, 7 121
St. Petersburg	L. M. 164
St. Petrox	L. M. 43
St Philip and St. James	L.M. 38
St. Sacrament	10 146
St. Thomas	S M. 186
St. Timothy	C. M. 120
Stillwater	11, 11 72
Stockwell	8, 7 3
Sullivan	12 101
Swabia	S. M. 29
Tantum Ergo	8, 7, 4 178
The Christian's Hiding Place	8,7 202
The Last Beam	P. M. 193
The Lord will Provide	H.M. 190
The Roseate Hues	C.M. D. 106
Tivoli	6, 4 17
Toplady	7,61 125
Tristes Erant	L. M. 80
Unser Herrscher	8, 7, 8, 7 81
Uxbridge	L. M. 6
Vigil	S. M. 155
Vigilate	7, 7, 7, 3 168
Vox Dilecti	C. M. D. 182
Ward	L. M. 110
Watchman	S.M. 70
Webb	7, 6 128
We Give Thee But Thine Own	S. M. 15
Wellesley	8, 7 87
White	11, 10 26
Whittier	L. M. 142
Williams	L. M. 142
Windsor	C. M. 25
Wonderful Words	148
Woodland	C.M. 173
Wordsworth	L.M. 111
Yoakley	L. M. 61 122

HYMNS AND TUNES
FOR
THE CHURCH OF CHRIST, SCIENTIST,

STOCKWELL. 8s & 7s.   D. E. JONES.

1. Hear our pray'r O gracious Fa-ther, Author of ce-les-tial good,
That thy laws so pure and ho-ly May be bet-ter un-der-stood.

2. As the dew before the sunlight;
Melts and fadeth from our sight,
So may every doubt and error
Fade before eternal light.

3. Armed with faith may we press onward
Knowing nothing but thy will,
Conquering every storm of error
With the sweet words, "Peace, be still."

4. Like the star of Bethlehem shining,
Love will guide us all the way,
From the depths of error's darkness,
Into Truth's eternal day.

FLOSSIE L. HEYWOOD.

GOD.

FIAT LUX. P. M.   *Hymns, Ancient and Modern.*

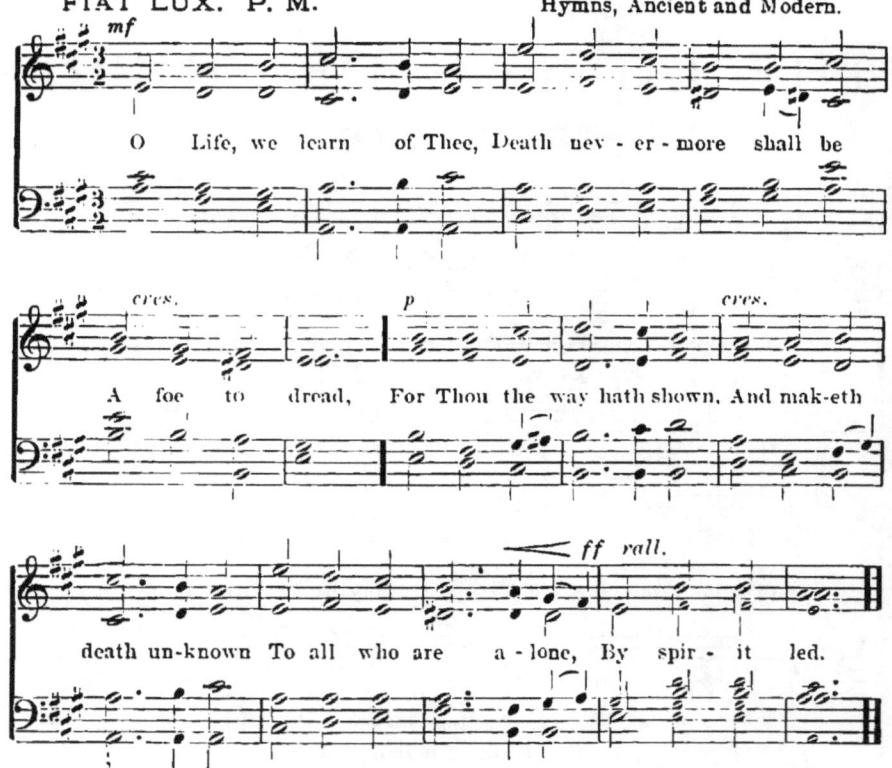

O Life, we learn of Thee, Death nev-er-more shall be A foe to dread, For Thou the way hath shown, And mak-eth death un-known To all who are a-lone, By spir-it led.

2 O Truth, Thy voice we hear,
  Still, small, distinct and clear,
    Bidding us take
  The path, where Thou hast walked.
  Though scorned, despised and mocked.
  For Thou to us hast talked,
    Our peace to make.

3 O Love Thy blessings shine,
  Pure, radiant, divine,
    Into our hearts;
And darkness flees away,
Before the brightening ray
  That ushers in the day;
    And fear departs.

4 O Life and Truth and Love,
  Blest Trinity above;
    All earthly fears,
We live alone in Thee.
And evermore shall be,
  From mortal toils, set free;
    And griefs and tears.

                     NELLIE B. EATON.

GOD.

1. Fear not, O little flock, the foe
Who madly seeks your overthrow;
Dread not his rage and power,
What tho' your courage sometimes faints?
This seeming triumph o'er God's saints
Lasts but a little hour.

2. Fear not, be strong! your cause belongs
To Him, who can avenge your wrongs;
Leave all to Him, your Lord;
Though hidden yet from mortal eyes,
Salvation shall for you arise;
He girdeth on his sword!

3. As true as God's own promise stands,
Not earth nor hell, with all their bands,
Against us shall prevail;
The Lord shall mock them from his throne;
God is with us; we are his own;
Our victory cannot fail!

GUSTAVUS ADOLPHUS, in prose. JACOB FABRICIUS.
Translated by Miss C. WINKWORTH.

UXBRIDGE. L. M.   LOWELL MASON.

1 Come, O Thou universal Good;
  Balm of the wounded conscience, come!
  Haven to take the shipwrecked in,
  My everlasting rest from sin.

2 Come O my comfort and delight!
  My strength, and health, and shield and sun,
  My boast, my confidence and might,
  My joy, my glory, and my crown.

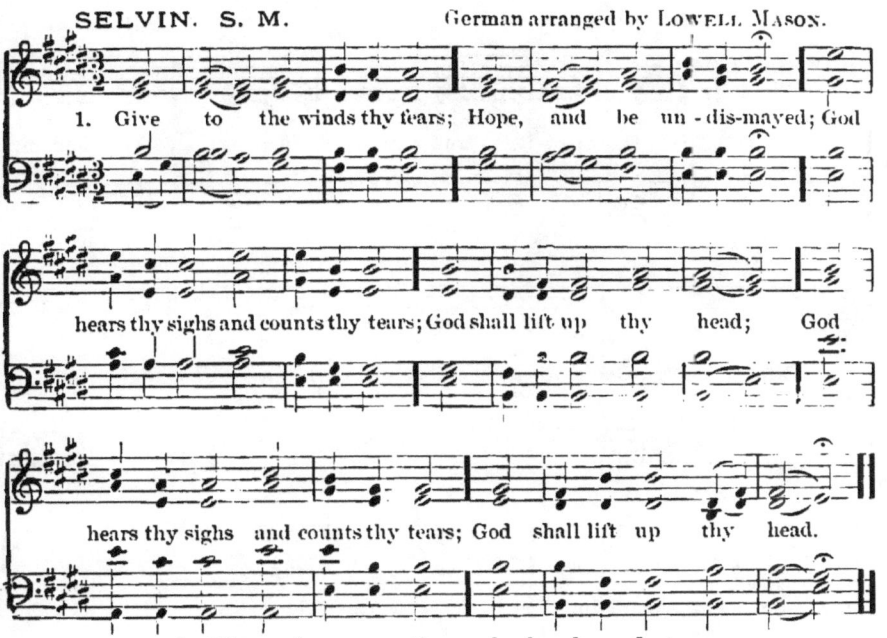

SELVIN. S. M.   German arranged by LOWELL MASON.

1. Give to the winds thy tears; Hope, and be un-dis-mayed; God hears thy sighs and counts thy tears; God shall lift up thy head; God hears thy sighs and counts thy tears; God shall lift up thy head.

2. Through waves, through clouds and storms.
 He gently clears thy way;
 Wait thou his time; so shall this night,
 Soon end in joyous day.

3. He everywhere hath sway,
 And all things serve his might:
 His every act pure blessing is,
 His path unsullied light.

4. Leave to his sovereign sway.
 To choose and to command:
 With wonder filled, thou then shalt own,
 How wise, how strong his hand.

5. Thou comprehend'st him not,
 Yet earth and heaven tell:
 God sits as Sovereign on the throne;
 He ruleth all things well.

PAUL GERHARDT, 1659.
Translated by JOHN WESLEY, 1739.

GOD.

HOPKINS. 9, 8.   E. J. HOPKINS.

1. In Thee O Spir-it true and ten-der, I find my life as God's own child; With-in Thy Light of glo-rious splen-dor, I lose the earth clouds drear and wild

2. In Thee I have no pain or sorrow,
   No anxious thought, no load of care;
   Thou art the same to-day, to-morrow,
   Thy Love and Truth are everywhere.

3. Within Thy Love, is safe abiding
   From every thought that giveth fear;
   Within Thy Truth, a perfect chiding,
   Should I forget that Thou art near.

4. Thy grace is all sufficient for me,
   The precious Life a perfect light;
   No evil thought can come before Thee,
   Thy mind is pure, Thy home is bright.

F. A. F.

LYONS. 10, 11. FRANCIS J. HAYDN.

1. Tho' troubles as-sail, and dan-gers af-fright, Tho' friends should all fail, and foes all u-nite, Yet one thing se-cures us, what-ev-er be-tide, The promise as-sures us, "The Lord will pro-vide."

2. The birds, without barn or store-house, are fed;
From them let us learn to trust for our bread:
His saints what is fitting shall ne'er be denied,
So long as 'tis written, "The Lord will provide."

3. When Satan appears to stop up our path,
And fills us with fears, we triumph by faith;
He cannot take from us, tho' oft he has tried,
The heart cheering promise, "The Lord will provide."

4. He tells us we're weak, our hope is in vain;
The good that we seek we ne'er shall obtain;
But when such suggestions our graces have tried,
This answers all questions, "The Lord will provide."

JOHN NEWTON.

NEARER TO THEE. 6, 4.

CHAS. BEECHER.

1. Nearer, my God, to thee! Nearer to thee, E'en though it be, a cross That raiseth me; Still all my song shall be Nearer, my God, to thee! Nearer to thee!

2 Though like the wanderer,
  The sun gone down,
 Darkness be over me,
  My rest a stone,
 Yet in my dreams I'd be
 Nearer, my God, to thee,
  Nearer to thee!

3 There let the way appear,
  Steps unto heaven;
 All that thou sendest me,
  In mercy given;
 Angels to beckon me
 Nearer, my God, to thee,
  Nearer to thee!

4 Then, with my waking tho'ts
  Bright with thy praise,
 Out of my stony griefs
  Bethel I'll raise;
 So by my woes to be
 Nearer, my God, to thee,
  Nearer to thee!

5 Or if, on joyful wing
  Cleaving the sky,
 Sun, moon, and stars forgot
  Upward I fly,
 Still all my song shall be,
 Nearer, my God, to thee,
  Nearer to thee!

MRS. SARAH F ADAMS.

2. Workman of God! O lose not heart,
   But learn what God is like;
   And in the darkest battle-field,
   Thou shalt know where to strike.

3. Muse on his justice, downcast soul,
   Muse, and take better heart;
   Back with thine angel to the field,
   And bravely do thy part.

4. For right is right, since God is Good.
   And right the day must win;
   To doubt would be disloyalty,
   To falter would be sin.

   DUNDEE.

GOD.

AVON. C. M. — Hugh Wilson.

1 The thought I have my ample creed,
  So deep it is and broad,
And equal to my ev'ry need,
  It is the thought of God.

2 Each morn unfolds some fresh surprise,
  I feast at life's full board;
And rising in my inner skies,
  Shines forth the thought of God.

3 At night my gladness is my prayer,
  I drop my daily load;
And every care is pillowed there,
  Upon the thought of God.

4 I ask not far before to see
  But take, in trust, my load;
Love, Truth, and immortality,
  Are in my thought of God.

5 To this their secret strength they owed,
  The martyrs path who trod;
The fountains of their patience flowed,
  From out their thought of God.

2 Holy Spirit, Love divine!
  Glow within this heart of mine;
  Kindle every high desire;
  Perish self in thy pure fire!

3 Holy Spirit, Right divine!
  King within my conscience reign;
  Be my law, and I shall be
  Firmly bound, forever free.

4 Holy Spirit Joy divine!
  Gladden thou this heart of mine;
  In the desert ways I sing,
  Spring O Well, forever spring.

                    CHAS. WESLEY,
                    SAMUEL LONGFELLOW.

14   GOD.

ERNAN. L. M.   Lowell Mason.

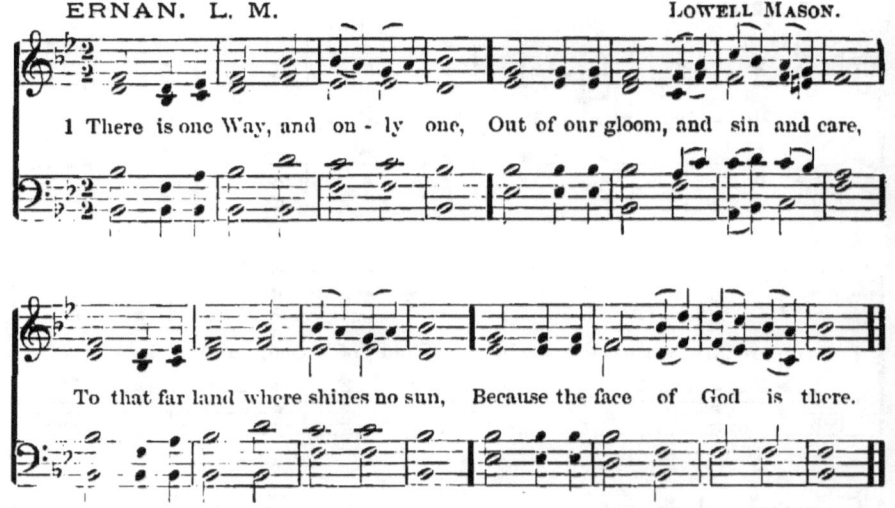

1 There is one Way, and on-ly one, Out of our gloom, and sin and care, To that far land where shines no sun, Because the face of God is there.

    2 There is one Truth, and that is God,
      That Christ revealed on Earth to show,
      One Life that His redeeming blood
      Has won for all mankind below.

    3 The lore from Philip once concealed,
      We know its fulness now in Christ;
      In Him the Father is revealed,
      And all our longing is sufficed.

    4 And still unwavering faith holds sure
      The words that James wrote sternly down;
      Except we labor and endure.
      We cannot win that heavenly crown.

    5 O Way divine, through gloom and strife
      Bring us our Father's face to see;
      O heavenly Truth, O precious Life,
      At last, at last, we rest in Thee.

WE GIVE THEE BUT THY OWN. S. M.

We give Thee but Thine own, What-e'er the gift may be;
All that we have is Thine a-lone, A trust, O Lord, from Thee.

2 May we Thy bounties thus
  As stewards true receive,
And gladly, as Thou blessest us,
  To Thee our first-fruits give.

3 The captive to release,
  To God the lost to bring,
To teach the way of life and peace,
  It is a Christ-like thing.

4 And we believe Thy Word,
  Though dim our faith may be;
Whate'er for Thine we do, O Lord,
  We do it unto Thee.

5 All might, all praise be Thine,
  Father, Co-equal Son,
And Spirit, bond of love Divine,
  While endless ages run.

CHRISTMAS. C. M.

Geo. Frederick Handel.

1. I cannot walk in darkness long, My Light is by my side; I cannot stumble or go wrong, While following such a guide, While following such a guide.

2. He is my stay and my defense,
   How shall I fail or fall?
   My keeper is Omnipotence;
   ‖: My Ruler ruleth all. :‖

3. The powers below and powers above,
   Are subject to his care;
   I cannot wander from his love,
   ‖: Whose love is everywhere. :‖

Caroline A. Mason.

TIVOLI. 6, 4. E. J. HOPKINS.

1 Word whose cre-a-tive thrill, Wakes in all na-ture still. Life, light and bloom; Come with re-sist-less ray, Chase all our clouds a-way And with thy heaven-ly day, All sense il-lume.

2 Spirit in whom we live,
Thou who dost yearn to give,
   All hearts thy rest;
When earthly joys take flight,
Cheer thou the earthly night,
And in the morning light,
   Still be our guest.

3 And when the eternal morn,
From death's deep night shades born,
   Our eyes shall see;
Father, thy word, thy breath.
Thy Christ, who conquereth
Sorrow and sin and death,
   Our trust shall be.

CHAS. T. BROOKS, 1873.

GOD.

ALMSGIVING. 8, 8, 8, 4.

1 O Lord of heaven, and earth, and sea, To Thee all praise and glory be; How shall we show our love to Thee, Who givest all?

2 The golden sunshine, vernal air,
Sweet flowers and fruit, Thy love declare;
When harvests ripen, Thou art there,
    Who givest all.

3 For peaceful homes, and healthful days,
For all the blessings earth displays,
We owe Thee thankfulness and praise,
    Who givest all.

4 Thou didst not spare Thine Only Son,
But gav'st Him for a world undone,
And freely with that Blessed One
    Thou givest all.

5 Thou giv'st the Holy Spirit's dower,
Spirit of life, and love and power,
And dost His sevenfold graces shower
    Upon us all.

6 To Thee, from Whom we all derive
Our life, our gifts, our power to give:
O may we ever with Thee live,
    Who givest all.

2 Spirit of glory and of God!
  Long hast Thou deigned my guide to be;
  Now be thy comfort sweet bestowed;
  My God! I come, I come to Thee.

3 I come to join that countless host
  Who praise thy name unceasingly;
  Blest Father, Son, and Holy Ghost!
  My God! I come, I come to Thee.
                                        Unknown.

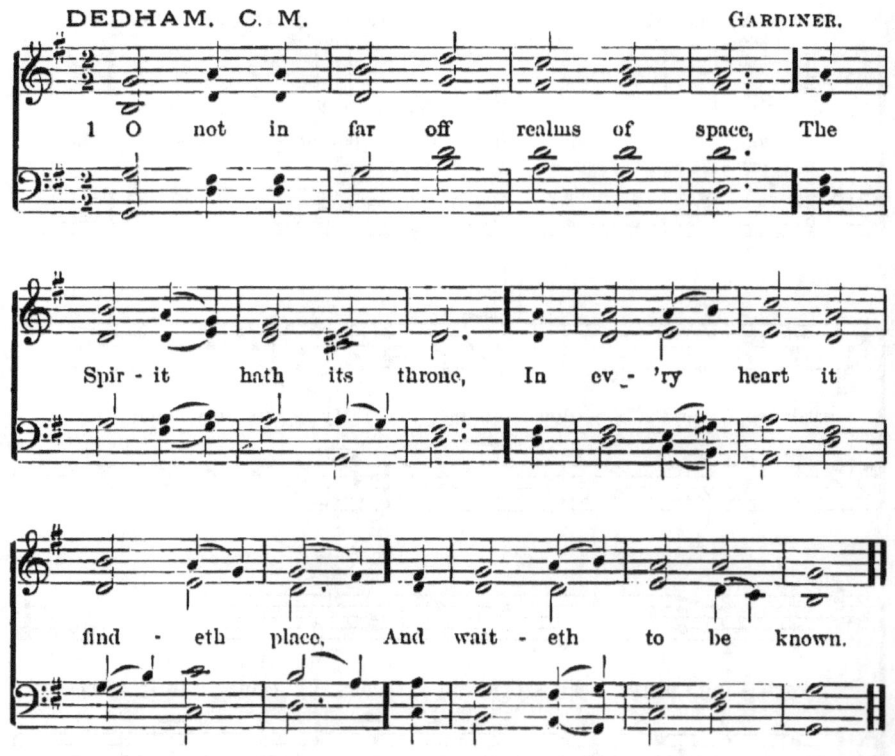

2 Thought answereth alone to thought,
And soul with soul hath kin;
The outward God, he findeth not,
Who finds not God within.

3 And if the vision come to Thee,
Revealed by inward sign;
Earth will be full of Deity,
And with His glory shine.

Anon.

2 'Tis Jesus, the first and the last,
  Whose Spirit shall guide us safe home;
  We'll praise Him for all that is past,
  And trust Him for all that's to come.

3 Our Father Almighty, to Thee
  We turn as our solace above;
  The waters may fail from the sea,
  But never Thy fountain of Love.
                                    JOSEPH HART

ARMENIA. C. M. — Sylvanus Billings Pond.

1 O Thou eternal fount of love,
   Ruler of nature's scheme,
   In Substance One and Christ with thee
   Omniscient and Supreme.

2 For Thy dear mercy's sake receive
   The strains and tears we pour;
   And purify our hearts to taste
   Thy sweetness more and more.

3 Our flesh, our reins, our spirits, Lord,
   In Thy clear fire refine;
   Break down the self-indulgent will,
   Gird us with strength divine.

1 Hamonious Principle, ours ever-more
Intelligence infinite, Thee we adore;
Thou ever art present, ever supreme,
Heaven of Spirit that will foil matter's dream.

2 Give us understanding of Truth and of Love,
We learn God, and Truth will all error remove;
Lead us to the Life, that is Soul unconfined,
Deliver from error untrue and unkind.

3 For Thou art the Life, that no death ever knew,
Thou Truth in such glory, no sin can be true,
Thou Love over all, and the infinite whole,
Forever and ever the Day Spring of Soul.

GOD.

MARA. C. M.

1. I trace your lines of ar-gue-ment, Your log-ic linked and strong; I weigh as one who dreads dis-sent, And fears a doubt as wrong.

2 Yet in the maddening maze of things,
  And tossed by storm and flood,
 To one fixed stake my spirit clings,
  I know that God is good.

3 The wrong that pains my soul below,
  I dare not throw above;
 I know not of His hate—I know
  His goodness and His love.

WHITTIER.

2 What heart can comprehend Thy name,
Or searching, find Thee out;
Who art within a quickening flame,
A presence round about.

3 Oh, dearer than all things, we know,
The child-like faith shall be;
That makes the darkest way we go
An open path to Thee.

Frederick L. Hosmer.

26   GOD.

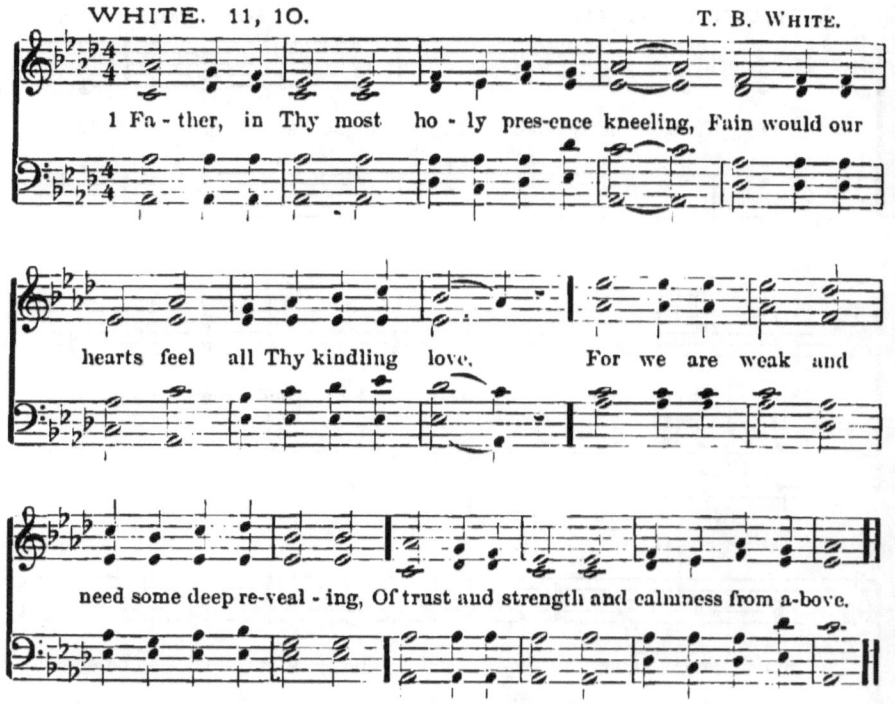

WHITE. 11, 10.   T. B. WHITE.

1 Father, in Thy most holy presence kneeling, Fain would our hearts feel all Thy kindling love, For we are weak and need some deep reveal-ing, Of trust and strength and calmness from above.

2 Lord, we have wandered forth through doubt and sorrow,
   And Thou hast made each step an onward one;
  And we will ever trust each unknown morrow,
   Thou wilt sustain us till our work is done.

3 In the heart's depths, a peace serene and holy,
   Abides; and when pain seems to have its will,
  Or dark despair, oh, may that peace rise slowly,
   Stronger than the evil, and we be still.

4 Now, Father, in thy dear presence kneeling,
   Our senses yearn to feel thy saving Love,
  O make us strong, we need Thy deep revealing,
   Of Faith and strength and calmness from above.
                                 SAMUEL JOHNSON.

1 Everlasting arms of love
  Are beneath, around, above;
  God it is who bears us on,
  His the arm we lean upon.

2 He our ever present guide,
  Faithful is whate'er betide;
  Gladly, then, we journey on,
  His the arm we lean upon.
                    Unknown.

2 If I am right, Thy grace impart,
  Still in the right to stay;
  If I am wrong, O teach my heart
  To find the better way.

3 This day be bread and peace my lot,
  All else beneath the sun,
  Thou knowest if bestowed or not,
  And let Thy will be done.
                        ALEXANDER POPE

2 To scorn the senses' sway,
   While still to Thee I tend;
   In all I do, be Thou the way;
   In all, be Thou the end.

3 All may of Thee partake;
   Nothing so small can be,
   But draws, when acted for Thy sake,
   Greatness and worth from Thee.

GOD.

PERCY. L. M.   H. P. Smith.

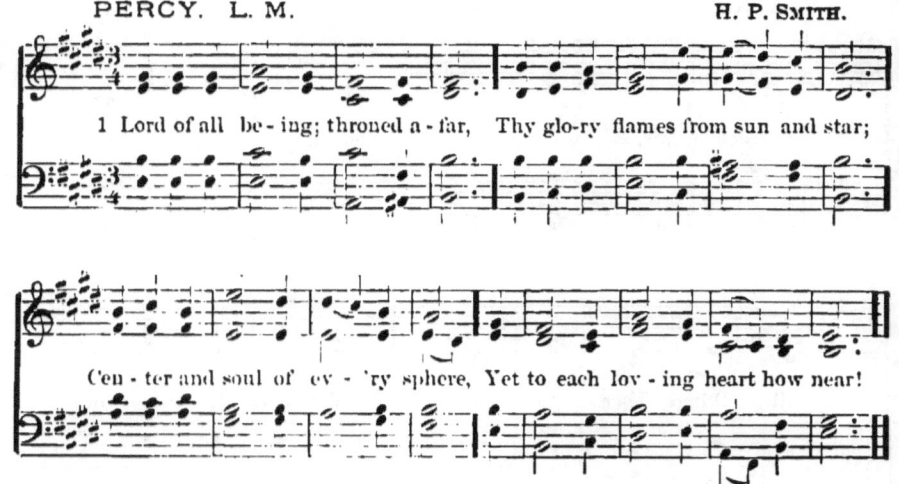

1 Lord of all be-ing; throned a-far, Thy glo-ry flames from sun and star; Cen-ter and soul of ev-'ry sphere, Yet to each lov-ing heart how near!

2 Sun of our life, Thy quickening ray
Sheds on our path the glow of day;
Star of our hope, thy softened light
Cheers the long watches of the night.

3 Our midnight is Thy smile withdrawn;
Our noontide is Thy gracious dawn;
Our rainbow arch Thy mercy's sign;
All, save the clouds of sin, are Thine.!

4 Lord of all life, below, above,
Whose light is truth, whose warmth is love,
Before thy ever-blazing throne
We ask no luster of our own,

5 Grant us Thy truth to make us free,
And kindling hearts that burn for Thee,
Till all the living altars claim
One holy light, one heavenly flame!

O. W. Holmes.

GOD. 31

LUX BENIGNA. 10, 4, 10. JOHN BACCHUS DYKES.

1 Lead, kindly Light, amid the encircling gloom, Lead Thou me on! The night is dark, and I am far from home, Lead Thou me on. Keep Thou my feet; I do not ask to see The distant scene; one step e-nough for me.

2 I was not ever thus, nor prayed that Thou
    Shouldst lead me on;
  I loved to choose and see my path; but now
    Lead Thou me on!
  I loved the garish day, and, spite of fears,
    Pride ruled my will. Remember not past years!

3 So long Thy power hath blest me, sure it still
    Will lead me on
  O'er moor and fen, o'er crag and torrent, till
    The night is gone,
  And with the morn those angel faces smile
  Which I have loved long since, and lost awhile!
                JOHN. H. NEWMAN.

32   GOD.

GENNESARET. 11.

1 See day-light is fad-ing o'er earth and o'er o-cean, The sun has gone down on the far dis-tant sea; Oh, now, in the hush of the fear-ful com-mo-tion, We lift our tired spir-its, blest Sav-ior, to Thee.

2 Full oft wast Thou found afar on the mountain,
    As eventide spread her dark wing o'er the wave;
Thou Son of the Highest and life's endless fountain,
    Be with us, we pray Thee, to bless and to save.

3 And oft as the tumult of life's heaving billow,
    Shall toss our frail bark driving wild o'er night's deep;
Let Thy healing wing be stretched over o'er pillow,
    And guard us from evil though Death watch our sleep.

4 To God, our great Father, whose throne is in heaven,
    Who dwells with the lowly and humble in heart;
To the Son and the Spirit all glory be given,
    One God ever blessed and praised, Thou art.

HEBER.

2 We feel Thy calm at evening's hour,
    Thy grandeur in the march of night;
  And, when the morning breaks in power,
    We hear Thy word, "Let there be light."

3 But higher far, and far more clear,
    Thee in man's spirit we behold;
  Thine image and Thyself are there
    The indwelling God, proclaimed of old
                  SAMUEL LONGFELLOW.

2 Far, far beneath, the noise of tempests dieth,
And silver waves chime ever peacefully;
And no rude storm, how fierce so-e'er it flieth,
Disturbs the Sabbath of that deeper sea.

3 So the heart that knows Thy love, O Purest!
There is a temple sacred evermore;
And all the babble of life's angry voices
Dies in hushed stillness at its peaceful door.

4 Far, far away, the roar of passion dieth,
And loving thoughts rise calm and peacefully,
And no rude storm how fierce so-e'er it flieth,
Disturbs the soul, that dwells, O Lord, in Thee.

5 O Rest of rests! O Peace serene, eternal!
Thou ever livest and Thou changest never;
And in the secret of Thy presence dwelleth
Fulness of joy for ever and ever.

Mrs. Stowe.

ARLINGTON. C. M.   Thos. Augustine Arne.

1 We pray no more, made lowly wise; For miracle and sign; Anoint our eyes to see within The common, the divine.

2 We turn from seeking Thee afar,
   And in unwonted ways,
   To build from out our daily lives
   The temples of Thy praise.

3 And if Thy casual comings, Lord,
   To hearts of old were dear,
   What joy shall dwell within the faith
   That feels Thee ever near.

4 And nobler yet shall duty grow
   And more shall worship be,
   When Thou art found in all our life,
   And all our life in Thee.
                      Anon.

SEYMOUR. 7. C. M. Von Weber, 1849.
Arr. by H. W. Greatorex.

1. Life of all that lives below,
Let Thy Spirit in us flow;
We do all our life receive
From Thee, in Thee ever live.

2. But for fuller life we pine,
Let us more receive of Thine;
Still for more on Thee we call,
Thou who fillest all in all.

3. Live we now in Thee; be fed
Daily with the living bread;
Into Thee our spirits grow;
Into us Thy Spirit flow.

4. While we feel the vital blood,
While Thy full and quickening flood
Through life's every channel rolls,
Soul of all believing souls.

PORTUGUESE HYMN. 11.   JOHN READING, 1760.

1 The Lord is my Shepherd, no want shall I know; I feed in green pas-tures, safe-folded I rest; He leadeth my soul where the still waters flow, Restores me when wand'ring, redeems when oppressed, Restores me when wand'ring, redeems when oppressed.

2 Through the valley and shadow of death though I stray,
Since Thou art my guardian, no evil I fear;
Thy rod shall defend me, Thy staff be my stay,
No harm can befall, with my comforter near.

3 In the midst of affliction my table is spread;
With blessings unmeasured my cup runneth o'er;
With perfume and oil Thou anointest my head;
Oh, what sahll I ask of Thy providence more?

4 Let goodness and mercy, my bountiful God,
Still follow my steps, till I meet Thee above;
I seek, by the path which my forefathers trod,
Through the land of their sojourn, Thy Kingdom of love,
JAMES MONTGOMERY, 1822.

ST. PHILIP and ST. JAMES. L. M.

1 Thou who art peace and u-ni-ty, Send down Thy mild pa-cif-ic Dove; We all shall then in one a-gree, And breathe the spir-it of Thy love.

2 We all shall think and speak the same
   Delightful lesson of thy grace,
One undivided Christ proclaim,
   And jointly glory in Thy praise.

3 O let us take a softer mold,
   Blended and gathered into Thee;
Under one Shepherd make one fold,
   Where all is love and harmony.

4 Regard Thine own eternal prayer,
   And send a peaceful answer down;
To us Thy Father's name declare,
   Unite and perfect us in one.

5 So shall the world believe and know
   That God hath sent Thee from above;
When Thou art seen in us below,
   And every one displays Thy love.

CHAS. WESLEY.

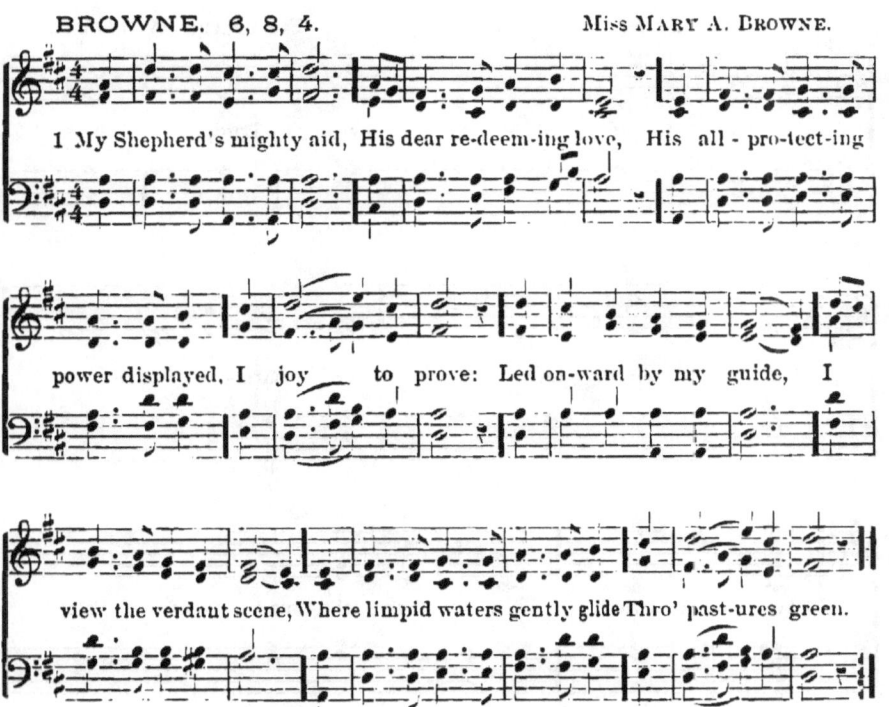

BROWNE. 6, 8, 4. Miss MARY A. BROWNE.

1 My Shepherd's mighty aid, His dear redeeming love, His all-protecting power displayed, I joy to prove: Led onward by my guide, I view the verdant scene, Where limpid waters gently glide Thro' pastures green.

2 In error's maze my soul
  Shall wander now no more;
His Spirit shall, with sweet control,
  The lost restore;
My willing steps shall lead
  In paths of righteousness;
His power defend; his bounty feed;
  His mercy bless.

3 Affliction's deepest gloom
  Shall but his love display;
He will the vale of death illume
  With living ray:
My failing flesh his rod
  Shall thankfully adore;
My heart shall vindicate my God
  For evermore.
                    THOMAS ROBERTS.

GOD.

DOVER. S. M. From AARON WILLIAMS.

1 Thy word, almighty Lord,
   Where'er it enters in,
  Is sharper than a two-edged sword,
   To slay the man of sin.

2 Thy word is power and life;
   It bids confusion cease,
  And changes envy, hatred, strife,
   To love, and joy, and peace.

3 Then let out hearts obey
   The gospel's glorious sound;
  And all its fruits, from day to day,
   Be in us and abound.
                    JAMES MONTGOMERY.

SAVIOR, LIKE A SHEPHERD. 8. 7. 4.   W. B. BRADBURY.

1 Yes, we trust the day is breaking,
   Joyful things are near at hand;
   God, the mighty God is speaking,
   By His work in every land;
      God is speaking,
   Darkness flies at His command.

2 With the voice of joy and singing,
   Let us hail the dawning ray;
   Lo! the blessed day-star bringing
   O'er the earth a glorious day;
      At His rising,
   Gloom and darkness flee away.

KELLEY.

42   GOD.

CREATION. L. M. D.   F. J. HAYDN.

1 My Lord, how full of sweet content,
  I pass my years of banishment!
  Where'er I dwell, I dwell with Thee,
  In heaven, on earth, or on the sea.
  To me remains nor place nor time;
  My country is in every clime:
  I can be calm and free from care
  On any shore, since God is there.

2 While place we seek, or place we shun,
  The soul finds happiness in none;
  But with a God to guide our way,
  'Tis equal joy, to go or stay.
  Could I be cast where Thou art not,
  That were indeed a dreadful lot;
  But regions none remote I call,
  Secure of finding God in all.

  Madam GUYON, 1702.
  Tr. by WM. COWPER, 1782.

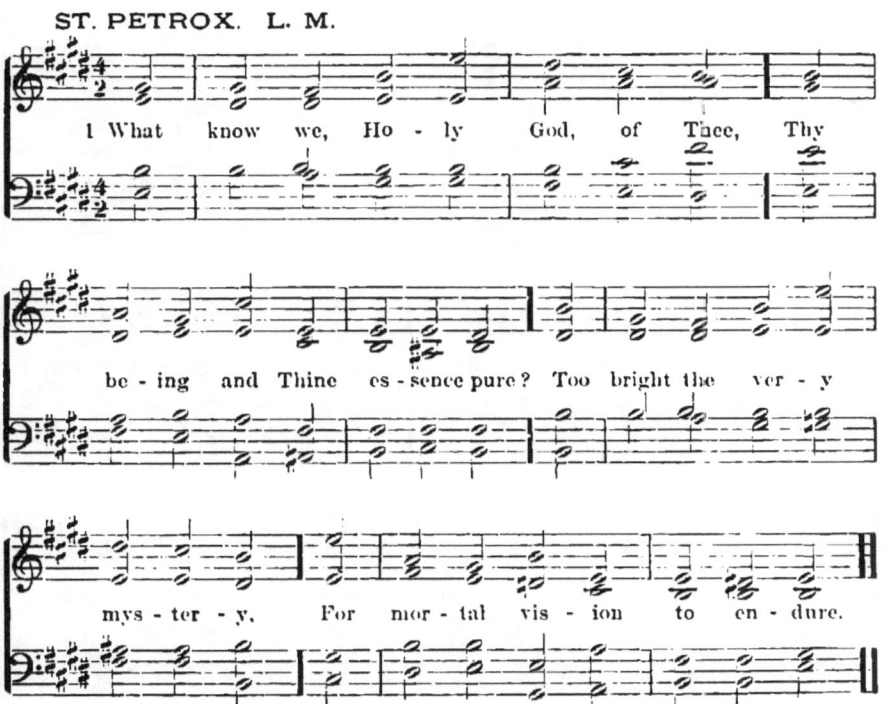

1 What know we, Holy God, of Thee,
  Thy being and Thine essence pure?
  Too bright the very mystery
  For mortal vision to endure.

2 We only know Thy word sublime,
  Thou art the Spirit! Perfect! One!
  Unlimited by space or time,
  Unknown but through the eternal Son.

3 By change untouched, by thought untraced,
  And by created eye unseen,
  In Thy great Present is embraced
  All that shall be, all that hath been.
                    FRANCES RIDLY HAVERGAL.

GOD.

AMSTERDAM. 7, 6, 7. JAMES NARES, 1760

1 Open, Lord, my inward ear,
    And bid my heart rejoice;
  Bid my quiet spirit hear
    The comfort of Thy voice,
  Never in the whirlwind found,
    Or where earthquakes rock the place;
  Still and silent is the sound,
    The whisper of Thy grace.

2 From the world of sin and noise,
    And hurry, I withdraw;
  For the small and inward voice
    I wait with humble awe;
  Silent I am now and still,
    Dare not in Thy presence move;
  To my waiting soul reveal
    The secret of Thy love.

CHAS. WESLEY, 1742.

FATHER MOST HOLY.   WILLIAM F. SHERWIN.

1 Father most holy! To whom all praise belongs; Thy children lowly To Thee would bring our songs. Praises nev-er end-ing, All harmonius blending, To Thy throne ascending, Swell from heav'nly tongues.

REFRAIN.
Lord we a-dore Thee! And with the Ser-a-phim Bow-ing be-fore Thee, Join in their holy hymn.

Copyright, 1885, by PHILLIPS & HUNT. Used by permission.

2 Jesus, our Savior,—
  Name more than all most sweet!
Seeking Thy favor,
  We worship at Thy feet.
All our sins confessing,
Thou our hearts possessing,
May Thy gracious blessing
  Here our spirits greet.   REF.

p Come, Holy Spirit,
  Kindle devotions fire!
By Thine own merit
  Our every thought inspire.

God's own word unsealing,
Precious truth revealing,
Thou canst bring the healing
  Sin-sick souls desire.   REF.

4 Thus do we bless Thee,
  O Thou great One in Three!
Gladly confess Thee,
  Our Lord and King to be.
Hallelujahs swelling,
Shall Thy praise be telling,
Till, with Jesus dwelling,
  We Thy glory see!   REF.

WM. F. SHERWIN.

THE DIVINE IDEA.

JESUS SHALL REIGN. L. M.   KARL WILHELM, Arr.

1 Jesus shall reign where'er the sun
Does his successive journeys run;
His kingdom spread from shore to shore,
Till moons shall wax and wane no more.
From north to south the princes meet,
To pay their homage at His feet,
While western empires own their Lord,
And savage tribes attend his word.

2 To Him shall endless prayer be made,
And endless praises crown his head;
His name like sweet perfume shall rise
With every morning sacrifice.
People and realms of every tongue
Dwell on His love with sweetest song,
And infant voices shall proclaim
Their early blessings on his name.

ISAAC WATTS.

THE DIVINE IDEA.

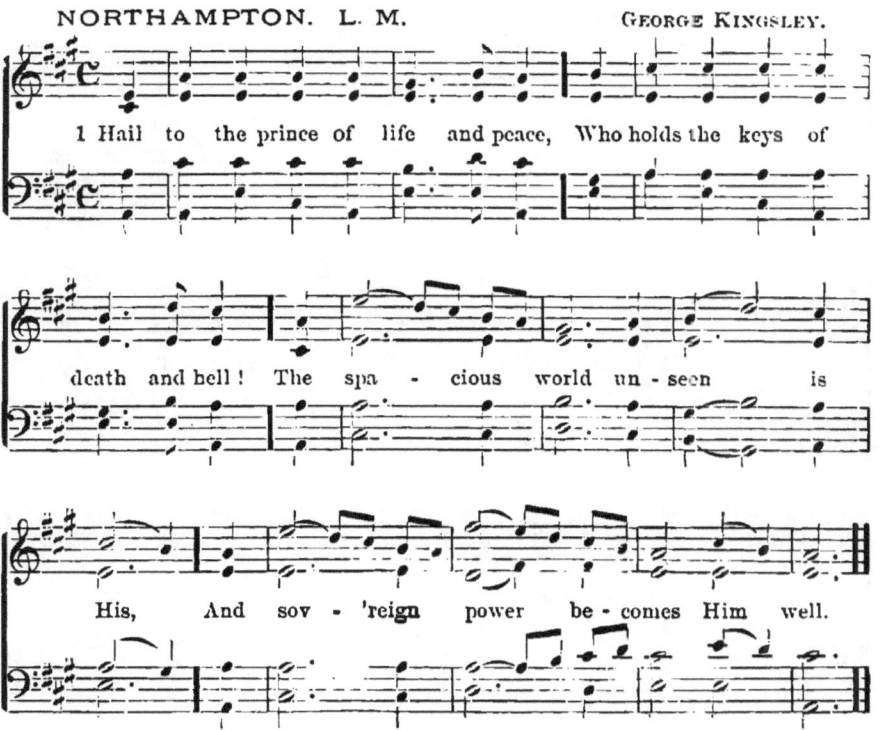

NORTHAMPTON. L. M.   GEORGE KINGSLEY.

1 Hail to the prince of life and peace, Who holds the keys of death and hell! The spacious world unseen is His, And sov-'reign power becomes Him well.

2 In shame and anguish once He died,
   But now He lives for ever-more;
   Bow down ye saints around His seat,
   And all ye angel-bands adore.

3 Worthy Thy hand to hold the keys,
   Guided by wisdom and by love;
   Worthy to rule o'er mortal life,
   O'er worlds below and worlds above.

4 Forever reign, victorious King,
   Wide through the earth Thy name be known;
   And call my longing soul to sing
   Sublimer anthems near Thy throne.

THE DIVINE IDEA.

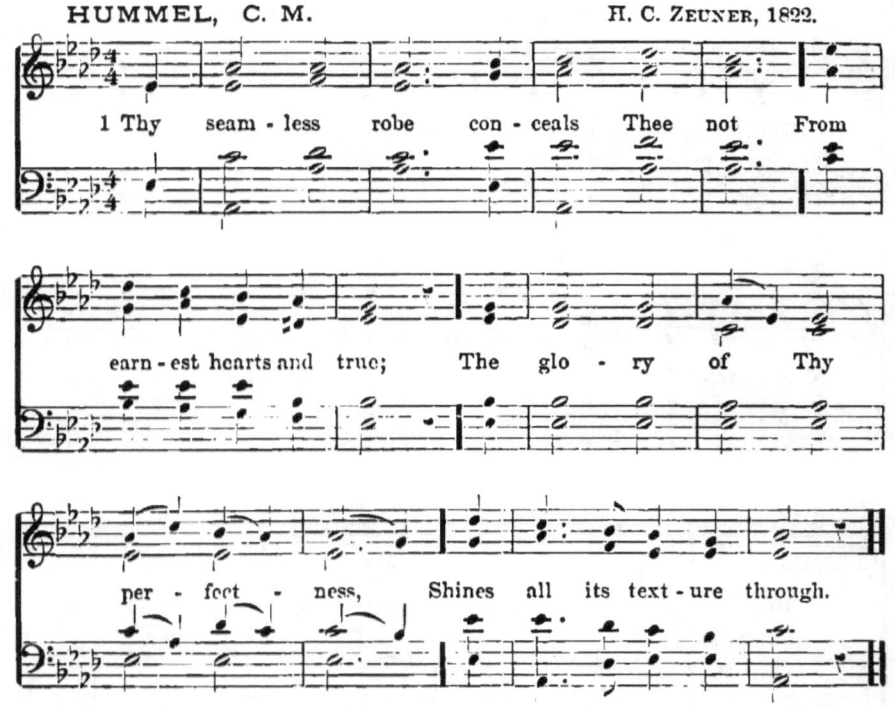

HUMMEL, C. M.   H. C. ZEUNER, 1822.

1 Thy seamless robe conceals Thee not
From earnest hearts and true;
The glory of Thy perfectness,
Shines all its texture through.

2 And on its flowing hem, we read,
As Thou dost linger near,
The message of a love more deep
Than any depth of fear.

3 And so no more our hearts shall plead,
For miracle and sign;
Thy order and Thy faithfulness,
Are all in all Divine.

4 These are Thy revelations vast
From earliest days of yore;
These are our confidence and peace,
We cannot wish for more.

JOHN W. CHADWICK, 1876.

THE DIVINE IDEA.

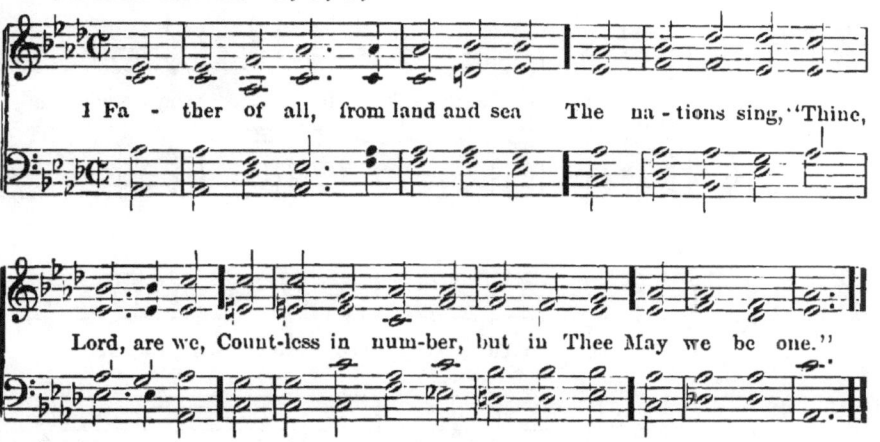

RISEHOLME. 8, 8, 8, 4.

1 Father of all, from land and sea
The nations sing, "Thine, Lord, are we,
Count-less in number, but in Thee
May we be one."

2 O Son of God, Whose love so free
  For men, did make Thee man to be,
  United to our God in Thee
    May we be one.

3 In Thee we are God's Israel,
  Thou art the world's Emmanuel,
  In Thee the saints forever dwell,
    Millions, but one.

4 Thou art the Fountain of all good,
  Cleansing with Thy most precious blood,
  And feeding us with Angel's Food,
    Making us one.

5 O Spirit blest, Who from above
  Cam'st gently gliding like a dove,
  Calm all our strife, give faith and love
    O make us one.

6 So, when the world shall pass away,
  May we awake with joy and say,
  "Now in the bliss of endless day
    We all are one."

THE DIVINE IDEA.

LOUVAN. L. M. VIRGIL CORYDON TAYLOR.

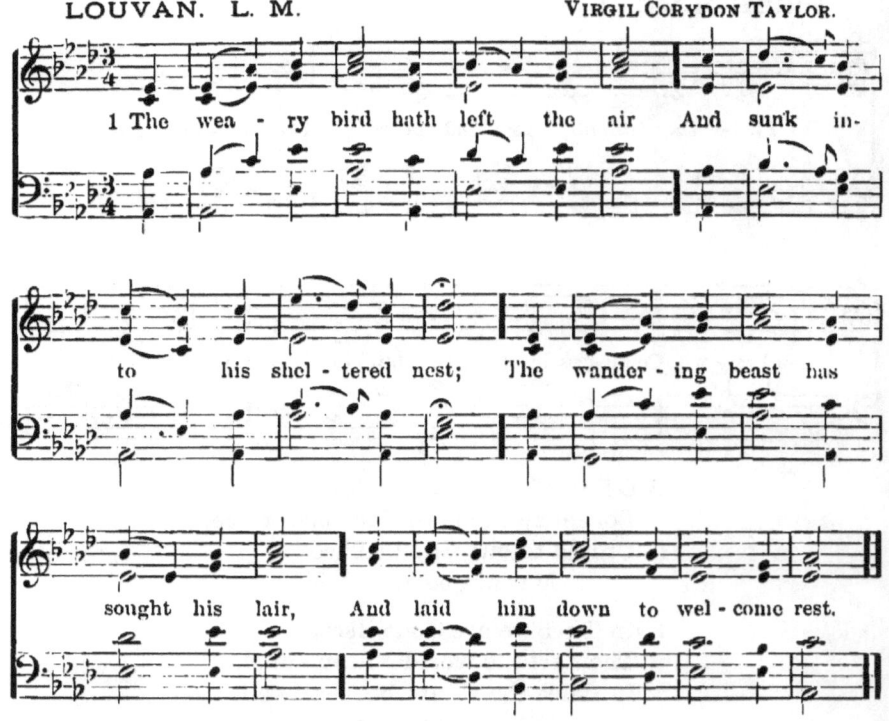

1 The wea-ry bird hath left the air And sunk in-to his shel-tered nest; The wander-ing beast has sought his lair, And laid him down to wel-come rest.

2 Still near the lake, with weary tread
   Lingers a form of human kind,
And on His lone, unsheltered head
   Flows the chill night-damp of the wind.

3 Why seeks He not a home of rest?
   Why seeks He not a pillowed bed?
Beasts have their dens, the bird its nest,
   He hath not where to lay His head.

4 Such was the lot He freely chose,
   To bless, to save the human race;
And through His poverty, there flows
   A rich, full stream, of heavenly grace.
                               RUSSELL.

THE DIVINE IDEA. 51

EVENING HYMN. L. M.   Thos. Tallis.

1 Jesus, Thou joy of loving hearts! Thou Fount of life! Thou Light of men! From the best bliss that earth imparts, We turn unfilled to Thee again.

2 Thy truth unchanged hath ever stood;
   Thou savest those that on Thee call;
   To them that seek Thee, Thou art good,
   To them that find Thee, All in all.

3 We taste Thee, O Thou Living Bread,
   And long to feast upon Thee still;
   We drink of Thee, the Fountain Head,
   And thirst our souls from Thee to fill!

4 Our restless spirits yearn for Thee,
   Where'er our changeful lot is cast;
   Glad, when Thy gracious smile we see,
   Blest, when our faith can hold Thee fast.
               Bernard of Clairvaux. Tr. by R. Palmer.

THE DIVINE IDEA.

BEETHOVEN. L. M.   Arr. by L. Mason.

1 "'Tis fin-ished!" so the Saviour cried, And meekly bowed His head and died: "'Tis fin-ished!" yes, the race is run, The battle fought, the vic-t'ry won.

2 'Tis finished! all that Heaven foretold
By prophets in the days of old;
And truths are opened to our view.
That kings and prophets sought to know.

3 'Tis finished! Son of God, Thy power
Hath triumphed in this awful hour;
And let our eyes Thy glory see
That death was captive led by Thee.

4 'Tis finished! let the joyful sound
Be heard by all the nations round;
'Tis finished! let earth's triumph rise,
And swell the chorus of the skies.
Samuel Stennett.

THE DIVINE IDEA. 53

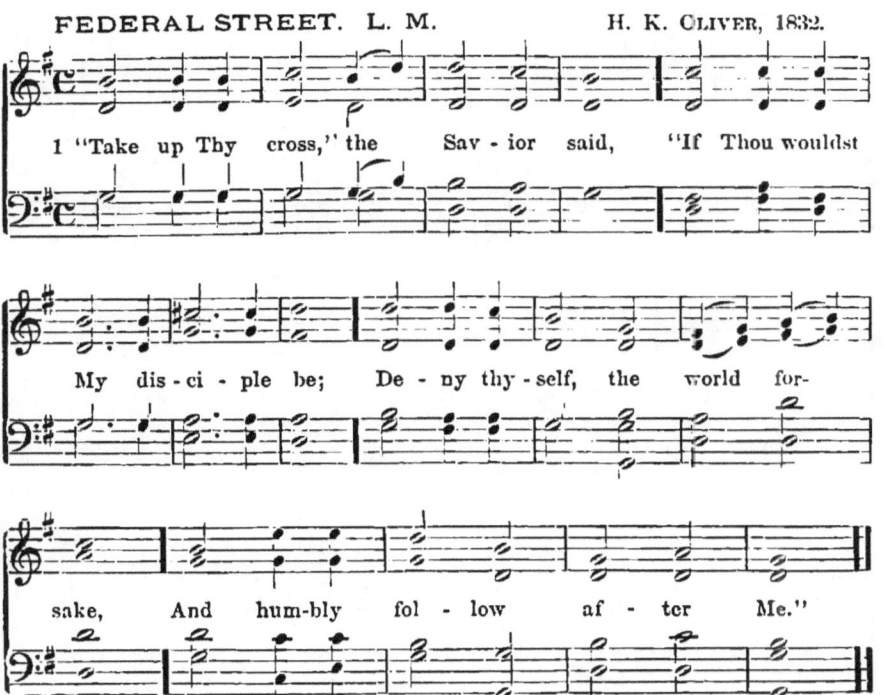

FEDERAL STREET. L. M.   H. K. OLIVER, 1832.

1 "Take up Thy cross," the Savior said, "If Thou wouldst My disciple be; Deny thyself, the world forsake, And humbly follow after Me."

2 "Take up thy cross," let not its weight
Fill thy weak spirit with alarm;
His strength shall bear thy spirit up,
And brace thy heart and nerve thine arm.

3 Take up thy cross, then, in His strength,
And calmly every danger brave;
'Twill guide thee to a better home,
And lead to victory o'er the grave.

4 Take up thy cross, and follow Christ,
Nor think till death to lay it down;
For only he who bears the cross
May hope to wear the glorious crown.
                               CHARLES W. EVEREST.

THE DIVINE IDEA.

GEER. C. M.
GEATOREX's Coll.

1 As shadows, cast by cloud and sun, Flit o'er the summer grass, So, in Thy sight, Almighty One, Earth's generations pass.

2 And while the years, an endless host,
   Come swiftly pressing on,
  The brightest names that earth can boast
   Just glisten and are gone.

3 Yet doth the star of Bethlehem shed
   A luster pure and sweet;
  And still it leads, as once it led,
   To the Messiah's feet.

4 O Father, may that holy star
   Grow every year more bright,
  And send its glorious beams afar
   To fill the world of light.
               WILLIAM C. BRYANT.

THE DIVINE IDEA. 55

AUTUMN. 8, 7, D.   Spanish Melody. From MARECHIO.

1 Know, my soul, thy full sal-va-tion; Rise o'er sin and fear and care;
Joy to find in ev-'ry sta-tion, Something still to do or bear;
D.S. Think what Je-sus did to win thee, Child of heav'n can'st thou re-pine.
Think what spir-it dwells with-in thee; Think what Fa-ther's smil-s are thine;

1 Know, my soul, thy full salvation;
   Rise o'er sin, and fear and care;
Joy to find in every station,
   Something still to do or bear;
Think what spirit dwells within thee;
   Think what Father's smiles are thine;
Think what Jesus did to win thee;
   Child of heaven, can'st thou repine?

2 Haste thee on from grace to glory,
   Arm'd with faith, and wing'd with prayer;
Heaven's eternal day before thee
   God's own hand shall guide thee there;
Soon shall close thine earthly mission,
   Soon shall pass thy pilgrim days;
Hope shall change to glad fruition,
   Faith to sight, and prayer to praise.
            HENRY FRANCIS LYTE, 1833.

THE DIVINE IDEA.

GOTTSCHALK. 7. — Louis Moreau Gottschalk.

1 Long ago in Holy Land, Lived there one by God's right hand; Nev-er ab-sent from God's sphere, Though He lived a-mong us here.

2 To His foll'wers gave the word,
They should still be with their Lord;
"Always I will be with you
Till this world be lost to view."

3 Light unto the world He brought,
Light the sages long had sought;
Light He gave of Life Divine,
Healing oil, and strength'ning wine.

4 Light was in Him, ever sure;
Light forever to endure;
Light with us will always be,
If the God of light we see.

S. C. R.

THE DIVINE IDEA.

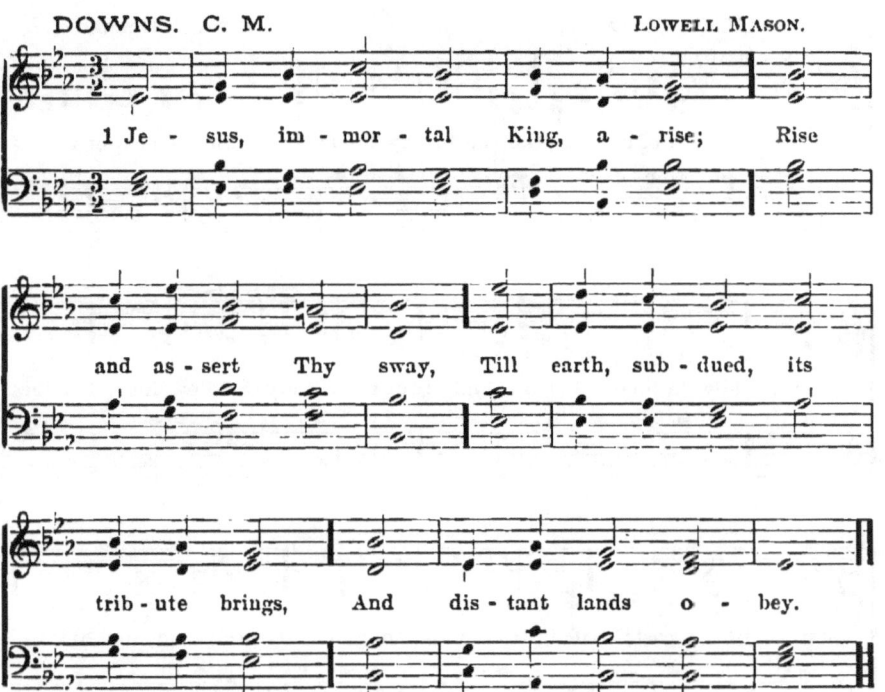

DOWNS. C. M.   LOWELL MASON.

1 Jesus, immortal King, arise;
  Rise and assert Thy sway,
  Till earth, subdued, its tribute brings,
  And distant lands obey.

2 Ride forth, victorious Conqueror, ride,
  Till all Thy foes submit,
  And all the powers of hell resign
  Their trophies at Thy feet.

3 Send forth Thy word, and let it fly
  The spacious earth around,
  Till every soul beneath the sun
  Shall hear the joyful sound.

4 From sea to sea, from shore to shore,
  May Jesus be adored,
  And earth, with all her millions, shout,
  Hosannas to the Lord.
                   BURDER.

THE DIVINE IDEA.

REFUGE. 7, D.   JOSEPH P. HOLBROOK.

1 Jesus, Lov-er of my soul, Let me to Thy bosom fly, While the near-er waters roll, While the tem-pest still is high! Hide me, O my Sav-ior, hide, Till the storm of life is past; Safe in-to the ha-ven guide, O receive my soul at last.

2 Other refuge have I none;
   Hangs my helpless soul on Thee:
 Leave, O leave me not alone,
   Still support and comfort me:
 All my trust on Thee is stayed,
   All my help from Thee I bring;
 Cover my defenseless head
   With the shadow of Thy wing!

3 Thou, O Christ, art all I want;
   More than all in Thee I find;
 Raise the fallen, cheer the faint,
   Heal the sick, and lead the blind.

Just and holy is Thy name,
   I am all unrighteousness:
False and full of sin I am,
   Thou art full of truth and grace.

4 Plenteous grace with Thee is found,
   Grace to cover all my sin.
 Let the healing streams abound:
   Make and keep me pure within.
 Thou of life the fountain art,
   Freely let me take of Thee:
 Spring thou up within my heart,
   Rise to all eternity.

                CHARLES WESLEY.

THE DIVINE IDEA

HAYDN. S. M. HAYDN.

1 Jesus, my Truth, my Way,
 My sure, unerring Light,
On Thee my feeble steps I stay,
 Which Thou wilt guide aright.

2 My Wisdom and my Guide,
 My Counselor Thou art;
O never let me leave Thy side,
 Or from Thy paths depart.

3 Never will I remove
 From out Thy hands my cause;
ut rest in Thy redeeming love,
 And hang upon Thy cross.

4 O make me all like Thee,
 Before I hence remove;
Settle, confirm, and 'stablish me,
 And build me up in love.

CHAS. WESLEY.

THE DIVINE IDEA.

BEATITUDO. C. M.

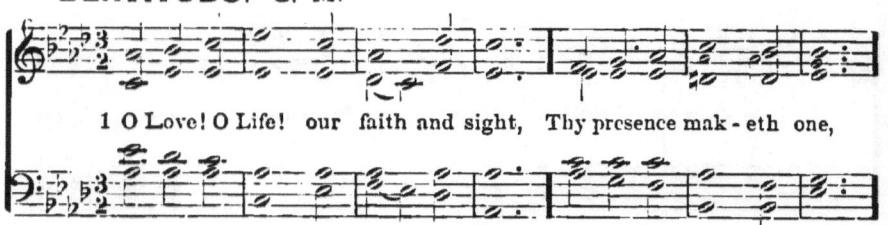

1 O Love! O Life! our faith and sight, Thy presence mak-eth one, As through transfigured clouds of white, We trace the noon-day sun.

2 So to our mortal eye subdued,
Flesh-veiled, but not concealed,
We know in Thee the father-hood,
And heart of God revealed.

3 We faintly hear, we dimly see,
In differing phrase we pray;
But dim or clear, we own in Thee,
The Life, the Truth, the Way.

4 To do Thy will is more than praise,
As words are less than deeds;
And simple trust can find Thy ways,
We miss with chart of creeds.

5 Our Friend, our Brother and our Lord,
What may Thy service be?
For name, nor form, nor ritual word,
But simply following Thee.

JOHN G. WHITTIER.

THE DIVINE IDEA. 61

JESHURUN. 7, 6, 7.   HENRY JOHN GAUNTLETT.

1 To the ha-ven of Thy breast, O Son of man, I fly; Be my refuge and my rest, For O the storm is high! Save me from the furious blast; A covert from the tem-pest be: Hide me, Je-sus, till o'er-past The storm of sin I see.

2 Welcome as the water-spring
  To a dry, barren place,
O descend on me, and bring
  Thy sweet, refreshing grace;
O'er a parched and weary land,
  As a great rock extends its shade,
Hide me Savior, with Thy hand,
  And screen my naked head.

3 In the time of my distress
  Thou hast my succor been·
In my utter helplessness,
  Restraining me from sin;
O how swiftly didst Thou move
  To save me in the trying hour!
Still protect me with Thy love,
  And shield me with Thy power.

CHAS. WESLEY.

THE DIVINE IDEA.

ANTIOCH. C. M.   From HANDEL.

2 Joy to the world! the Savior reigns;
   Let men their songs employ;
While fields and floods, rocks, hills, and plains,
   Repeat the sounding joy.

3 No more let sin and sorrow grow,
   Nor thorns infest the ground;
He comes to make His blessings flow
   Far as the curse is found.

4 He rules the world with truth and grace,
   And makes the nations prove
The glories of His righteousness,
   And wonders of his love.
                ISAAC WATTS.

GOD. 63

CHRIST CHURCH. H. M.   CHAS. STEGGALL.

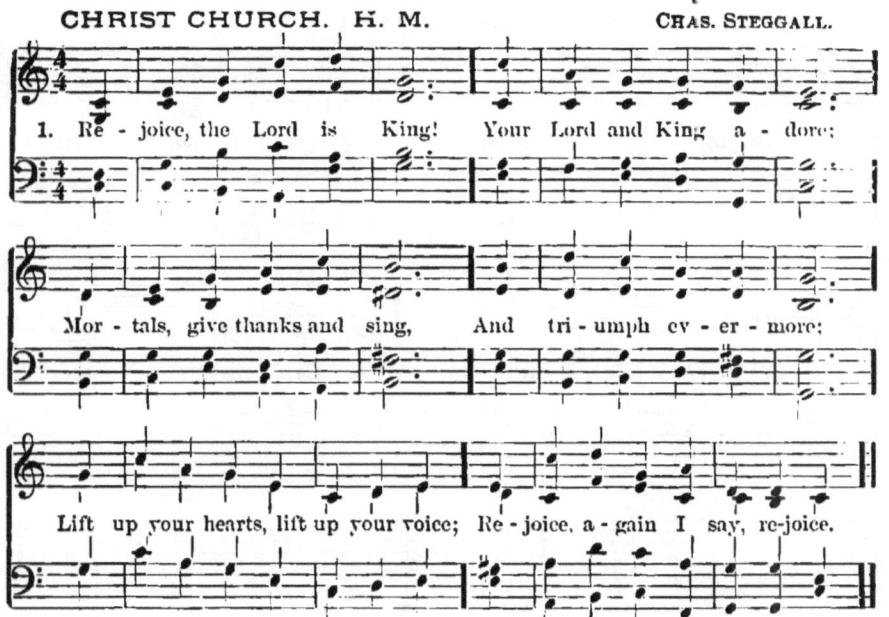

1. Re-joice, the Lord is King! Your Lord and King a-dore;
Mor-tals, give thanks and sing, And tri-umph ev-er-more;
Lift up your hearts, lift up your voice; Re-joice, a-gain I say, re-joice.

2. Jesus, the Savior, reigns,
 The God of truth and love;
When he had purged our stains,
 He took his seat above:
Lift up your hearts, lift up your voice;
Rejoice, again I say, rejoice.

3. His kingdom cannot fail,
 He rules o'er earth and heaven;
The keys of death and hell
 Are to our Brother given;
Lift up your hearts, lift up your voice;
Rejoice, again I say, rejoice.

4. He sits at God's right hand,
 Till all his foes submit,
And bow to his command,
 And fall beneath his feet:
Lift up your hearts, lift up your voice;
Rejoice, again I say, rejoice.

CHAS. WESLEY.

CHRISTMAS.

SEMPER ASPECTEMUS. C. M.

1 Bright was the guiding star that led,
   With mild, benignant ray,
The Gentiles to the lowly bed
   Where the Redeemer lay.

2 But lo! a brighter, clearer light
   Now points to his abode;
It shines through sin and sorrow's night,
   To guide us to our God.

3 O Gladly tread the narrow path,
   While light and grace are given;
Who meekly follow Christ on earth
   Shall reign with him heaven.

HARRIET AUBER.

CHRISTMAS.

HERMANN. C. M.   N. HERMANN.

1 To us a Child of hope is born, To us a Son is given; Him shall the tribes of earth o-bey, Him, all the hosts of heav'n.

2 His name shall be the Prince of peace,
   For evermore adored;
The Wonderful, the Counselor,
   The great and mighty Lord!

3 His power increasing, still shall spread;
   His reign no end shall know:
Justice shall guard His throne above
   And peace abound below.

4 To us a Child of hope is born,
   To us a Son is given;
The Wonderful, the Counselor,
   The mighty Lord of heaven.
                     JOHN MORRISON.

CHRISTMAS.

BETHLEHEM. 8, 6.   ENGLISH.

1 O little town of Bethlehem! How still we see thee lie, Above thy deep and dreamless sleep, The silent stars go by; Yet in thy dark streets shineth The everlasting Light; The hopes and fears of all the years, Are met in thee to-night.

2 For Christ conceived of Mary,
  Has garnered all above,
While mortals sleep the angels [keep
  Their watch of wondering love.
O morning stars together
  Proclaim the holy birth!
And praises sing to God the King,
  And peace to men on earth.

3 How silently, how silently,
  The wondrous gift is given;
So God imparts to human hearts
  The blessings of his heaven.

No ear may hear his coming,
  But in this world of sin, [still,
Where meek souls will receive him
  The dear Christ enters in.

4 O holy child of Bethlehem!
  Descend to us, we pray,
Cast out our sin and enter in,
  Be born in us to-day.
We hear the Christmas angels,
  The great glad tidings tell,
O, come to us, abide with us,
  Our Lord Emmanuel!
                    Unknown.

CHRISTMAS. 67

CHRISTMAS EVE. H. M.   J. ZUNDELL.

1 Hark! what celestial sounds, What music fills the air! Soft warbling to the morn, It strikes the ravished ear; Now all is still; Now wild it floats In tuneful notes, Loud, sweet and shrill.

2 Th' angelic hosts descend,
   With harmony divine;
See how from heaven they bend,
   And in full chorus join:
"Fear not," say they; | Jesus, your King,
"Great joy we bring;" | Is born to-day.

3 "He comes, your souls to raise
   From death's eternal gloom;
To realms of bliss and light
   He lifts you from the tomb:
Your voices raise, | Your songs unite
With sons of light; | Of endless praise.

4 "Glory to God on high;
   Ye mortals, spread the sound,
And let your raptures fly
   To earth's remotest bound;
For peace on earth, | To man is given,
From God in heaven | At Jesus' birth."

                                      SALISBURY Coll.

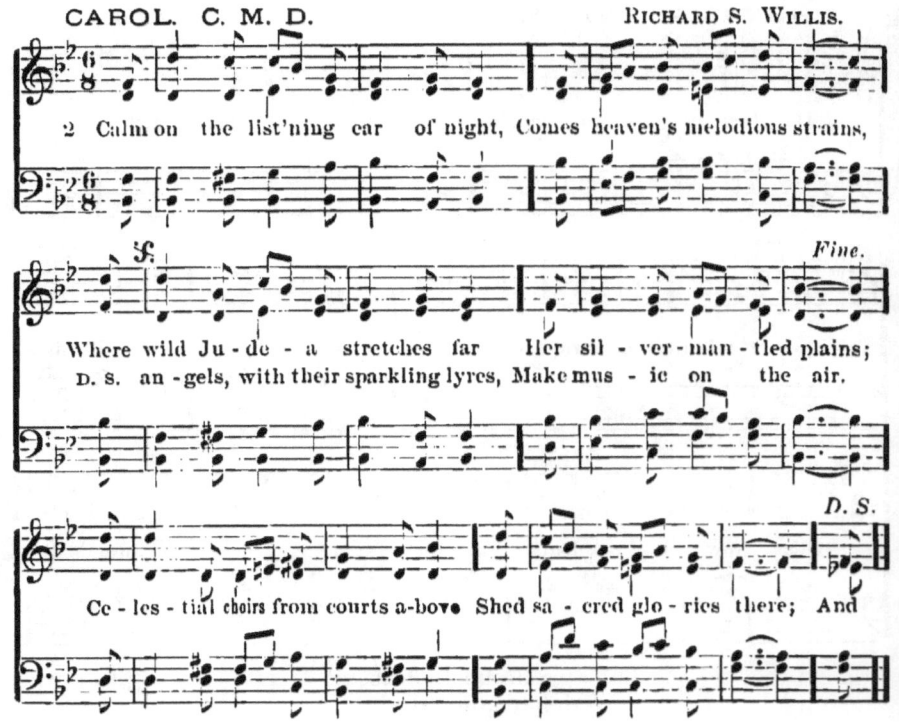

2 The answering hills of Palestine
  Send back the glad reply,
  And greet from all their holy heights
    The Dayspring from on high:
  O'er the blue depths of Galilee
    There comes a holier calm;
  And Sharon waves in solemn praise
    Her silent groves of palm.

3 "Glory to God!" the lofty strain
    The realm of ether fills;
  How sweeps the song of solemn joy
    O'er Judah's sacred hills!
  "Glory to God!" the sounding skies
    Loud with their anthems ring:
  "Peace on the earth; good-will to men,
    From heaven's eternal King."

EDMUND H. SEARS.

ST. AGATHA. 8, 7. R. S. T.

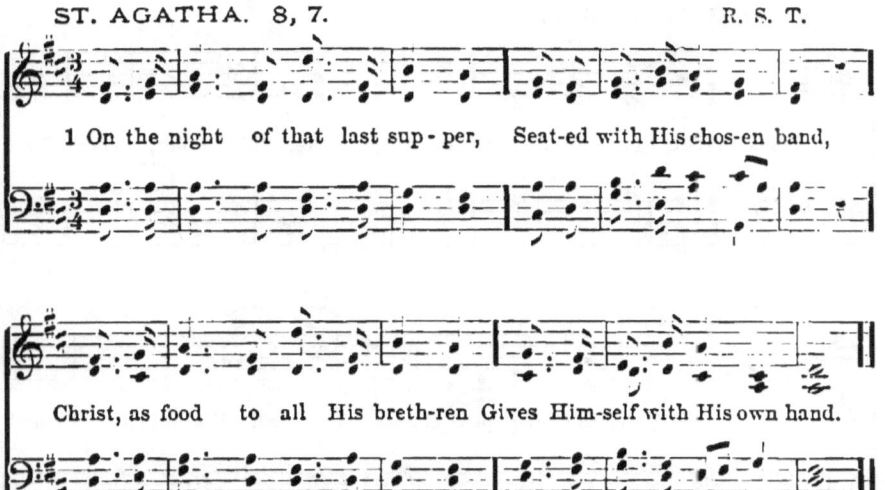

1 On the night of that last supper,
   Seated with His chosen band,
   Christ, as food to all His bretheren,
   Gives Himself, with His own hand.

2 He as man with man conversing,
   Staid the seeds of life to sow;
   Then He closed in solemn order,
   Wondrously, His life of woe.

3 Lo! o'er ancient forms departing,
   Newer rites of grace prevail;
   Faith for all defects supplying
   Where the feeble senses fail.

4 To the everlasting Father,
   Through the Son, Who reigns on high,
   Be all glory, honor, blessing,
   Might, and endless majesty.

BREVIARY.

COMMUNION.

WATCHMAN. S. M.

1 The Spirit, in our hearts,
   Is whispering, "Sinner, come."
 The bride, the Church of Christ, proclaims
   To all His children, "Come!"

2 Let him that heareth say
   To all about him, "Come!"
 Let him that thirsts for righteousness,
   To Christ, the Fountain, come!

3 Yea, whosoever will,
   O let him freely come,
 And freely drink the stream of life;
   'Tis Jesus bids him come.

4 Lo! Jesus, who invites,
   Declares, "I quickly come;"
 Lord, even so! we wait Thine hour:
   O blest Redeemer, come!

H. U. ONDERDONK.

COMMUNION.

EDDY. P. M. — WILLIAM HARRISON SMITH.

1 Calls out of darkness, the voice of the Lord,
   List to its notes soft and clear;
   Sick ones will lose all their pains,
   Sinners be rid of their stains,
      For the words of compassion thy hear.

2 Shines out of darkness the face of the Lord,
   With soft light, radiant and pure,
   Mourning ones dry all their tears,
   Timid ones cast off their fears,
      Of comfort and pity so sure.

3 See! out of darkness, the hand of the Lord,
   Beck'ning a lost world to come,
   Fainting ones they become bold,
   Infants grasp with tiny hold,
      And are led to the beautiful home.

G. B. DAY.

COMMUNION.

STILL WATER. 11, 11.

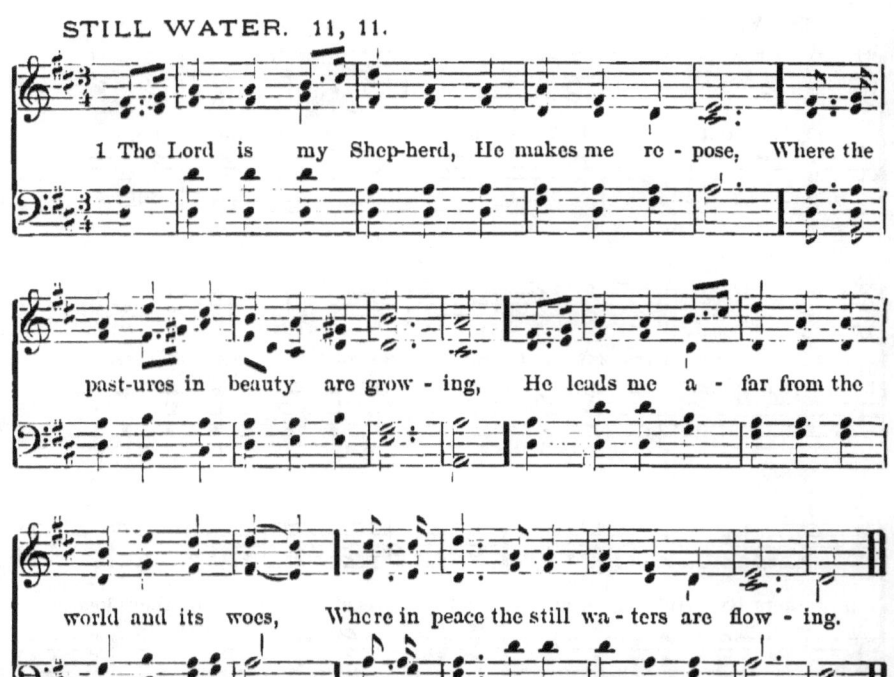

1 The Lord is my Shep-herd, He makes me re - pose, Where the past-ures in beauty are grow - ing, He leads me a - far from the world and its woes, Where in peace the still wa - ters are flow - ing.

2 He strengthens my spirit, He shows me the way,
Where the arms of His love shall enfold me;
And when I walk through the dark valley of death,
His rod and His staff will uphold me.

2 In the midst of affliction my table is spread;
With blessings unmeasured my cup runneth o'er;
With perfume and oil Thou anointest my head;
O what shall I ask of Thy providence more?

3 Let goodness and mercy, my bountiful God,
Still follow my steps till I meet Thee above;
I seek—by the path which my forefathers trod,
Through the land of their sojourn—Thy kingdom of love.

JAS. MONTGOMERY.

COMMUNION. 73

PARK STREET. L. M.   FREDRICK M. A. VENUA.

1 When on the mid-night of the East,
At the dead mo-ment of re-pose,
Like hope on mis-'ry's dark-ened breast,
The plan-et of sal-va-tion rose,
The plan-et of sal-va-tion rose.

2 The shepherd, leaning o'er his flock,
Started with broad and upward gaze,
Kneeled, while the star of Bethlehem broke
On music wakened into praise.

3 Shall we for whom that star was hung
In the dark vault of frowning heaven,
Shall we, for whom that strain was sung,
That song of peace and sin forgiven?

4 Shall we, for whom the Savior bled,
Careless, His banquet's blessing see,
Nor heed the parting word that said,
"Do this in memory of Me?"

74   COMMUNION.

KEBLE. L. M.

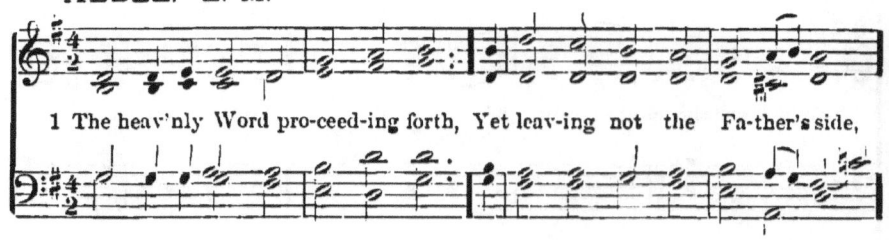

1 The heav'nly Word pro-ceed-ing forth, Yet leav-ing not the Fa-ther's side,

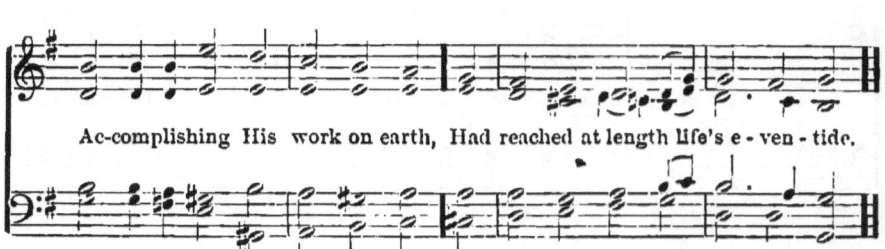

Ac-complishing His work on earth, Had reached at length life's e-ven-tide.

2 By false disciple to be given
   To foemen for His life athirst,
Himself, the very Bread of Heaven
   He gave to His disciples first.

2 He gave Himself in either kind,
   His precious Flesh, His precious Blood;
In love's own fulness thus designed
   Of the whole man to be the Food.

3 By Birth their Fellow-man was He;
   Their Meat, when sitting at the Board
He came, their Ransomer to be;
   He ever reigns, their great Reward

4 All praise and thanks to Thee ascend
   For evermore, Blest One in Three;
Life, Truth and Love, Thine own defend;
   We are Thine own in Unity.

SALSBURGH. 7, D. SEBASTIAN BACH.

1 At the Lambs' high feast we sing
Praise to our vic-to-rious King,
Who hath washed us in the tide
Flow-ing from His wound-ed side;
Praise we Him, Whose love di-vine
Gives His sa-cred blood for wine,
Gives His bod-y for the feast,
Christ the Vic-tim and the Priest.

2 Where the paschal blood is poured,
Death's dark angel sheathes his sword;
Isarel's hosts triumphant go
Thro' the waves that drowns the foe.
Praise we Christ, Whose blood was shed
Living Victim, Living Bread;
With sincerity and love
Eat we manna from above.

3 Mighty Victor from the sky!
Hell's dark powers beneath Thee lie;
Thou hast conquered in the fight,
Shown the way to Life and Light;
Hymns of glory, hymns of praise
Risen Lord, to Thee we raise;
Holy Father, Praise to Thee,
In the Spirit, ever be.

Tr. by R. CAMPBELL.

EASTER.

ST. HILDA. 7, 6. Rev. H. Husband.

1 The day of res-ur-rect-ion, Earth, tell it all a-broad! The pass-o-ver of glad-ness, The pass-o-ver of God! From death to life e-ter-nal, From this to life on high; The Christ hath brought us safely, With shouts of vic-to-ry.

2 Our hearts be pure from evil,
   That we may see aright
The Lord of life eternal,
   The resurrection light;
And, listening to His accents,
   May hear, so clear and plain,
His own "All hail!" and, hearing,
   Wake to new life again.

3 Now let the heavens be joyful!
   And earth her song begin!
Let all the world in triumph,
   O'er sickness, death, and sin!
Invisible and visible,
   Their notes of victory blend,
For Christ our Lord hath risen,
   Our Life that hath no end.

St. John of Damascus 380.

EASTER.

1 Lift your glad voices in triumph on high,
  For Jesus hath risen, and man cannot die;
Vain was the terrors that gathered around him,
  And short the dominion of death and the grave;
He burst from the fetters of darkness that bound Him,
  Resplendent in glory, to live and to save:
Loud was the chorus of angels on high,—
  The Savior hath risen, and man cannot die.

2 Glory to God, in full anthems of joy;
  The being He gave us, death cannot destroy:
Sad were the life we may part with to-morrow,
  If tears were our birthright, and death were our end;
But Jesus hath cheered the dark valley of sorrow,
  And bade us, immortal, to heaven ascend:
Lift then your glad voices in triumph on high,
  For Jesus hath risen, and man shall not die.
                              HENRY WARE, Jr.

EASTER.

FIRTH. P. M.   R. A. FIRTH.

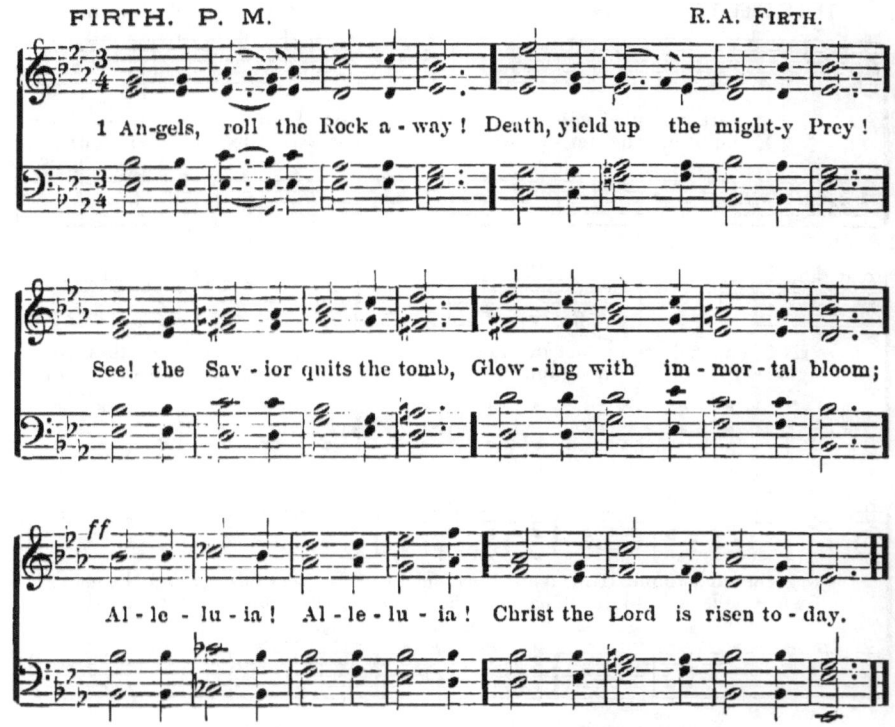

1 Angels, roll the Rock away! Death, yield up the mighty Prey!
See! the Savior quits the tomb, Glowing with immortal bloom;
Alleluia! Alleluia! Christ the Lord is risen to-day.

2 Shout ye seraphs angels, raise
Your eternal songs of praise;
Let the earth's remotest bound
Echo to the blissful sound.
   Alleluia! Alleluia!
Christ the Lord is risen to-day.

3 Holy Father, Holy Son,
Holy Spirit, Three in One,
Glory as of old to Thee,
Now and evermore shall be;
   Alleluia! Alleluia!
Christ the Lord is risen to-day.

                                             T. GIBBONS, 1784.

EASTER.

LOWRY. L. M.   J. E. SWEETSER,

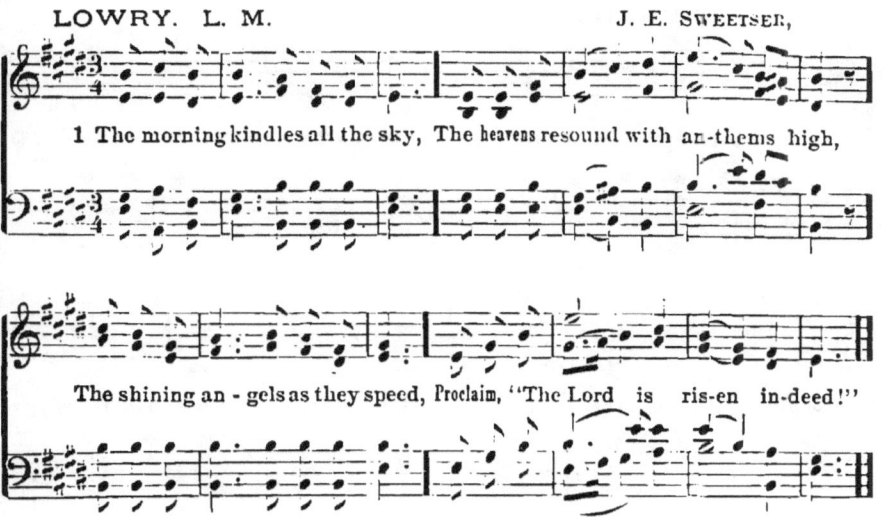

1 The morning kindles all the sky, The heavens resound with anthems high, The shining an-gels as they speed, Proclaim, "The Lord is ris-en in-deed!"

2 Vainly with rocks His tomb was barred,
While Roman guards kept watch and ward;
Majestic from the broken tomb,
In pomp and triumph, He has come!

3 When the amazed disciples heard,
Their hearts with speechless joy was stirred;
Their Lord's beloved face to see
Before Him haste to Galilee.

4 His wounded hands to them He shows,
His wondrous Love to thus disclose,
They with this glorious message speed,
"The Christ is risen, is risen indeed!"

5 O Christ, Thou King compassionate!
With Love, destroying death and hate:
With Thee we rise. if this we see,
And go before to Galilee!

                  Ambrosian, in the year, 550.

LOVE.

TRISTES ERANT. L. M.

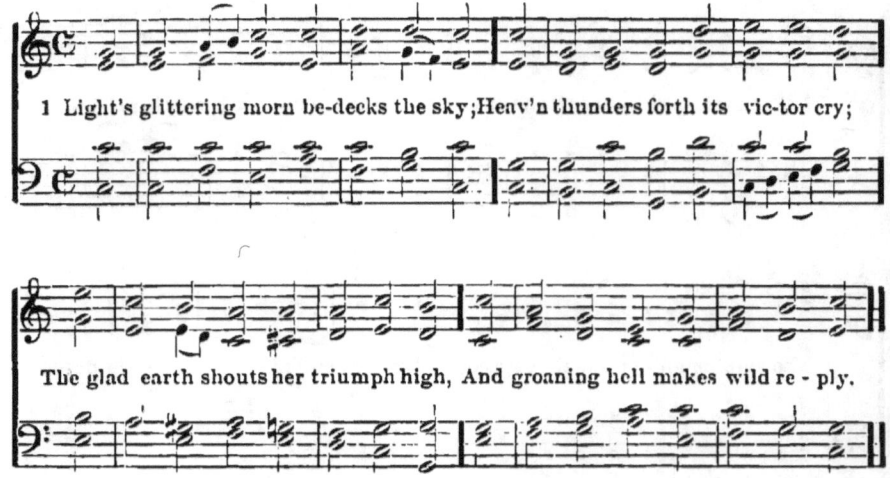

1. Light's glittering morn bedecks the sky;
   Heaven thunders forth its victor-cry;
   The glad earth shouts her triumph high,
   And groaning hell makes wild reply.

2. While He, the King, the mighty King,
   Despoiling death of all its sting,
   And, trampling down the powers of night,
   Brings forth His ransomed saints to light.

3. His tomb of late the threefold guard
   Of watch and stone and seal had barred·
   But now, in pomp and triumph high,
   He comes from death to victory.

4. The pains of hell are loosed at last;
   The days of mourning now are past;
   An Angel robed in light hath said,
   "The Lord is risen from the dead."

   Unknown.

EASTER.   81

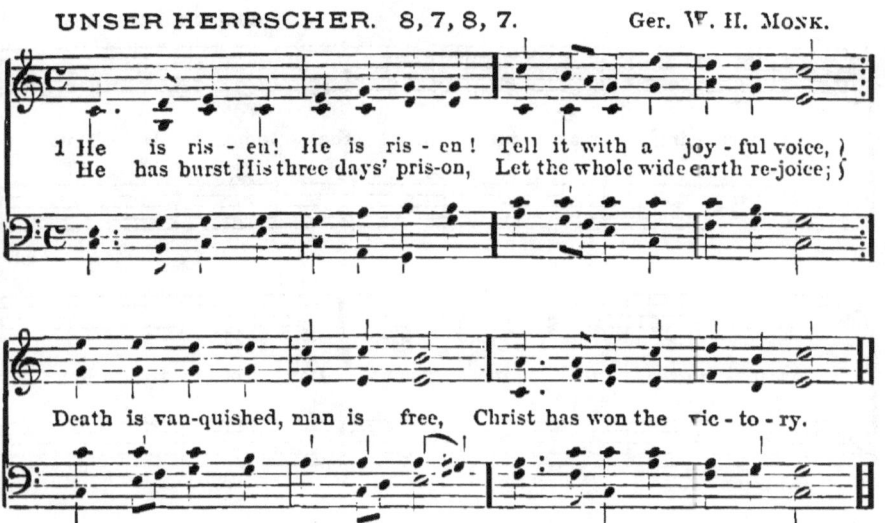

1 He is risen! He is risen!
    Tell it with a joyful voice,
  He has burst His three days' prison,
    Let the whole wide earth rejoice;
  Death is vanquished, man is free,
  Christ has won the victory.

2 Tell it to the sinners, weeping
    Over deeds in darkness done,
  Weary, fast and vigil keeping;
    Brightly breaks the Easter sun;
  Christ has borne our sins away,
  Christ has conquered hell to-day.

3 He is risen! He is risen!
    He has oped the eternal gate;
  We are loosed from sin's dark prison,
    Risen to a holier state,
  Where a brightening Easter beam,
  On our longing eye shall stream.

                              C. F. ALEXANDER. 1853.

EASTER.

HOLLEY. 7.
GEORGE HEWS, 1835.

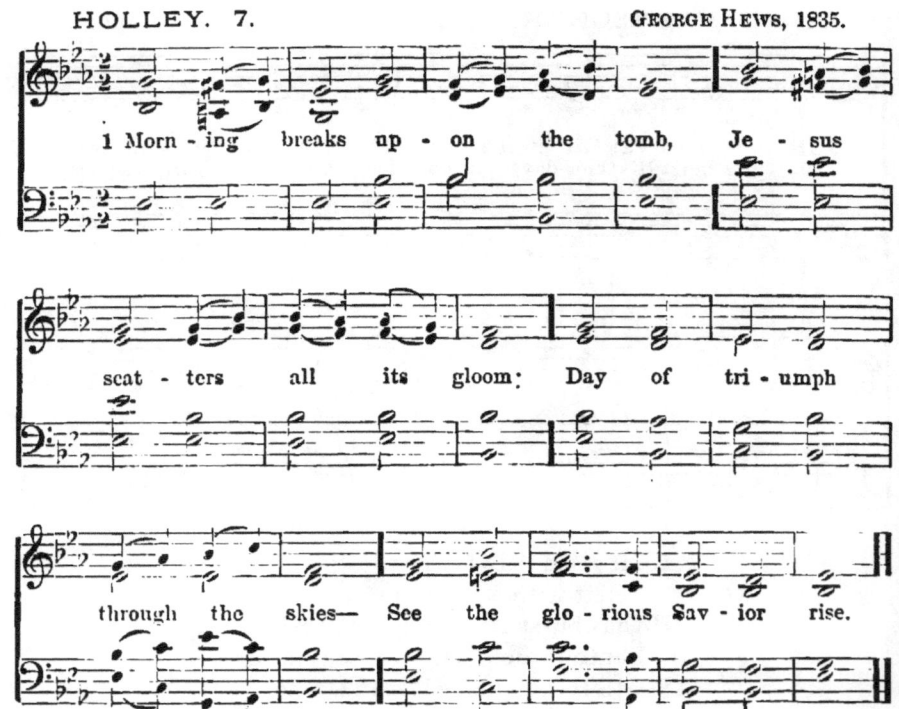

1 Morning breaks upon the tomb,
Jesus scatters all its gloom·
Day of triumph! Through the skies.—
See the glorious Savior rise!

2 Ye, who are of death afraid,
Triumph in the scattered shade;
Drive your anxious cares away;
See the place where Jesus lay!

3 Christian! dry your flowing tears,
Chase your unbelieving fears;
Look on His deserted grave;
Doubt no more His power to save.

COLLYER.

EASTER.

GREENWOOD. S. M.   JOSEPH E. SWEETSER.

1 The Lord is risen indeed;
     The grave hath lost its prey!
   With Him shall rise the ransomed seed,
     To reign in endless day.

2 The Lord is risen indeed;
     He lives, to die no more!
   He lives, his people's cause to plead,
     Whose curse and shame He bore.

3 The Lord is risen indeed;
     Attending angels, hear!
   Up to the courts of heaven, with speed,
     The joyful tidings bear:

4 Then take your golden lyres,
     And strike each cheerful chord;
   Join, all ye bright celestial choirs,
     To sing our risen Lord.
                   THOS. KELLY.

LOVE.

LINWOOD. L. M.   GIOACCHIMO ROSSINI.

1 O Love divine, that stooped to share Our sharpest pangs, our bitterest tear!

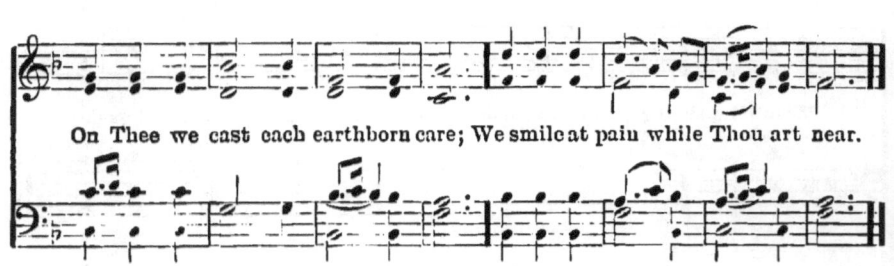

On Thee we cast each earthborn care; We smile at pain while Thou art near.

1 O Love divine, that stooped to share
    Our sharpest pang, our bitterest tear!
On Thee we cast each earthborn care;
    We smile at pain while Thou art near

2 Though long the weary way we tread,
    And sorrow crown each lingering year,
No path we shun, no darkness dread,
    Our hearts still whispering, "Thou art near!"

3 When drooping pleasure turns to grief,
    And trembling faith is changed to fear,
The murmuring wind, the quivering leaf,
    Shall softly tell us, "Thou art near!"

4 On Thee we fling our burdening woe,
    O Love divine, forever dear;
Content to suffer while we know,
    Living and dying, Thou art near!

OLIVER W. HOLMES.

LOVE.

PLEYEL'S HYMN. 7.
IGNACE PLEYEL.

1 Light of life, ser-aph-ic fire, Love di-vine, Thy-self im-part:
Ev-'ry faint-ing soul in-spire, En-ter ev-'ry droop-ing heart.

1 Light of life, seraphic fire,
　　Love divine, Thyself impart.
　Every fainting soul inspire,
　　Enter every drooping heart

2 Every mournful sinner cheer,
　　Scatter all our guilty gloom;
　Father! in Thy grace appear!
　　To Thy human temples come.

3 Come in this accepted hour!
　　Bring Thy heavenly kingdom in;
　Fill us with Thy glorious power,
　　Rooting out the seeds of sin.

4 Nothing more can we require,
　　We will covet nothing less;
　Be Thou all our heart's desire,
　　All our joy, and all our peace.
　　　　　　　　　　CHAS. WESLEY.

LOVE.

BERLIN. 10. MENDELSSOHN.

1 The suffering child with an unerring trust,
   Clings to the one who loves him most;
   The mother touch alone can still his cry,
   The mother love alone his needs supply.

2 How oft have we, children of riper years,
   Longed to regain the trust that calms all fears,
   Grown wise in error's ways, our trusts then seem
   As baseless as the fabric of a dream.

3 Despairing hearts, the voice of Love calls clear:
   Turn to the Light; thy help, thy strengh is near
   Come as the child comes; by thy trusting, prove
   That God, the source of Life and Truth, is Love.

M. M. C. S. B.

LOVE. 87

WELLESLEY. 8, 7.   LIZZIE S. TOURJEE.

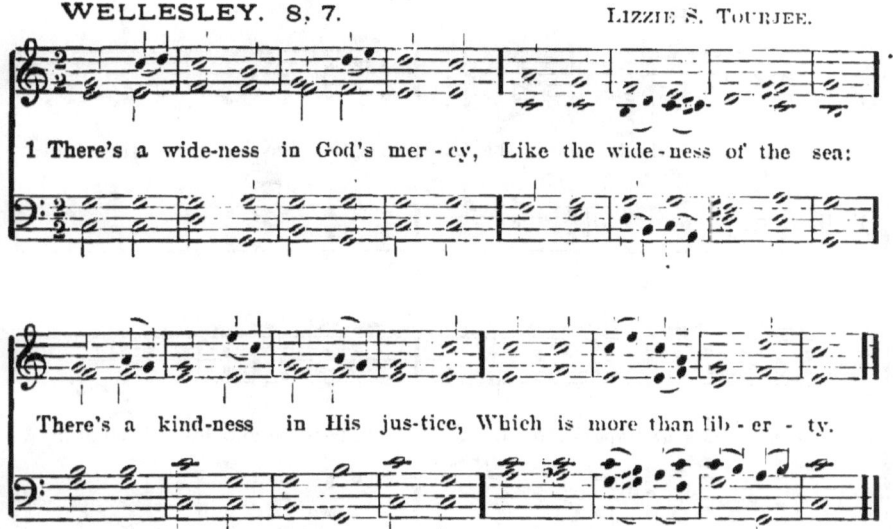

1 There's a wide-ness in God's mer-cy, Like the wide-ness of the sea:
There's a kind-ness in His jus-tice, Which is more than lib-er-ty.

1 There's a wideness in God's mercy,
   Like the wideness of the sea:
There's a kindness in His justice,
   Which is more than liberty.

2 There is welcome for the sinner,
   And more graces for the good;
There is mercy with the Savior;
   There is healing in His blood.

3 For the love of God is broader
   Than the measure of man's mind;
And the heart of the Eternal
   Is most wonderfully kind.

4 If our love were but more simple,
   We should take Him at His word;
And our lives would be all sunshine
   In the sweetness of our Lord.
                        F. W. FABER.

LOVE.

HYACINTH. 7.

1 Hark, my soul! it is the Lord; 'Tis thy Sav-ior, hear His Word; Je-sus speaks, and speaks to thee, "Say, poor sin-ner, lov'st thou Me?

2 "I delivered thee when bound,
And, when bleeding, healed thy wound;
Sought thee wandering, set thee right,
Turned thy darkness into light.

3 "Can a woman's tender care
Cease towards the child she bare?
Yes, she may forgetful be,
Yet will I remember thee.

4 "Mine is an unchanging Love,
Higher than the heights above,
Deeper than the depths beneath,
Overcoming fear of death.

4 "Thou shalt reach My glory soon,
When thy work of love is done;
Partner of My throne shalt be;
Say, poor sinner, lov'st thou Me?"

COWPER.

NIGHT THOUGHTS. L. M.

1 O fairest, born of Love and Light!
    Yet bending brow and eye severe,
  On all which pains Thy holy sight,
    Or wounds Thy pure and perfect ear;

2 Beneath Thy broad, impartial eye,
    How fade the lines of caste and birth;
  How equal in their sufferings lie,
    The groaning multitudes of earth!

3 In holy words which cannot die,
    In thoughts which angels leaned to know,
  Christ, give Thy message from on high,
    Thy mission to a world of woe.

4 That voice's echo hath not died;
    From the blue lake of Galilee,
  From Tabor's lonely mountain side
    It calls a struggling world to Thee.
                                WHITTIER.

LOVE.

LINWOOD. L. M.   GIOACCHIMO ROSSINI.

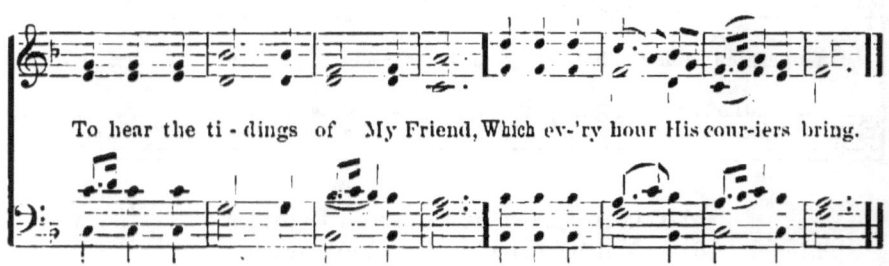

1 Love is and was my Lord and King,
  And in His presence I attend,
  To hear the tidings of my Friend,
  Which every hour His couriers bring.

2 Love is and was my King and Lord,
  And will be, though as yet I keep
  Within His court on earth to sleep,
  Encompassed by His faithful guard.

3 And hear at times a sentinel,
  Who moves about from place to place,
  And whispers to the worlds of space,
  In the deep night, that all is well.

                                TENNYSON.

LOVE.

BEMERTON. C. M.   H. W. GREATOREX.

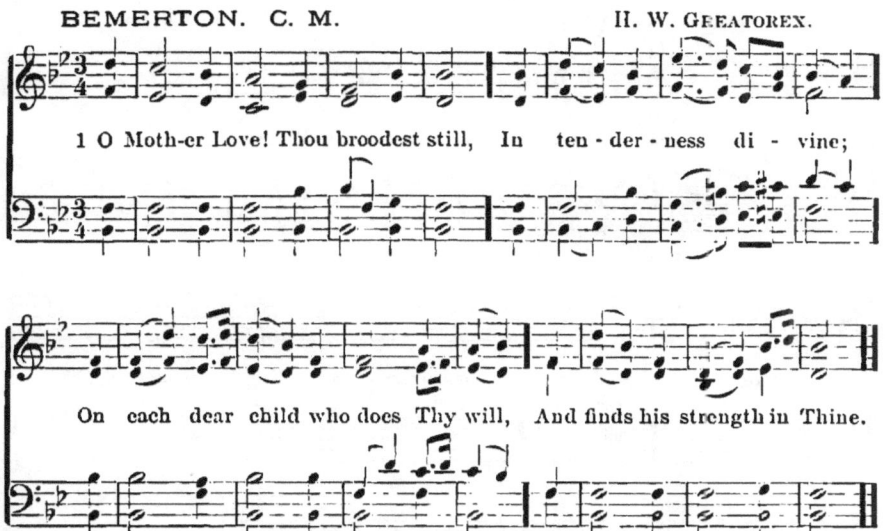

1 Oh Mother Love! Thou broodest still,
  In tenderness divine;
  On each dear child who does Thy will,
  And finds his strength in Thine.

2 The feathers of Thy bosom warm,
  His covering shall be,
  When snare of fowler waits to harm
  And shut him out from Thee.

3 The angels of Thy watchful care
  Are round about Thine own;
  They triumph over human fear,
  And trust in Thee alone.

4 When hatred flies its poisoned dart
  And clouds of terror lower,
  They nestle closer to Thy heart,
  Thy Truth their shield and power.

Ps. xci.   J. C. W.

LOVE.

COWPER. C. M.   LOWELL MASON.

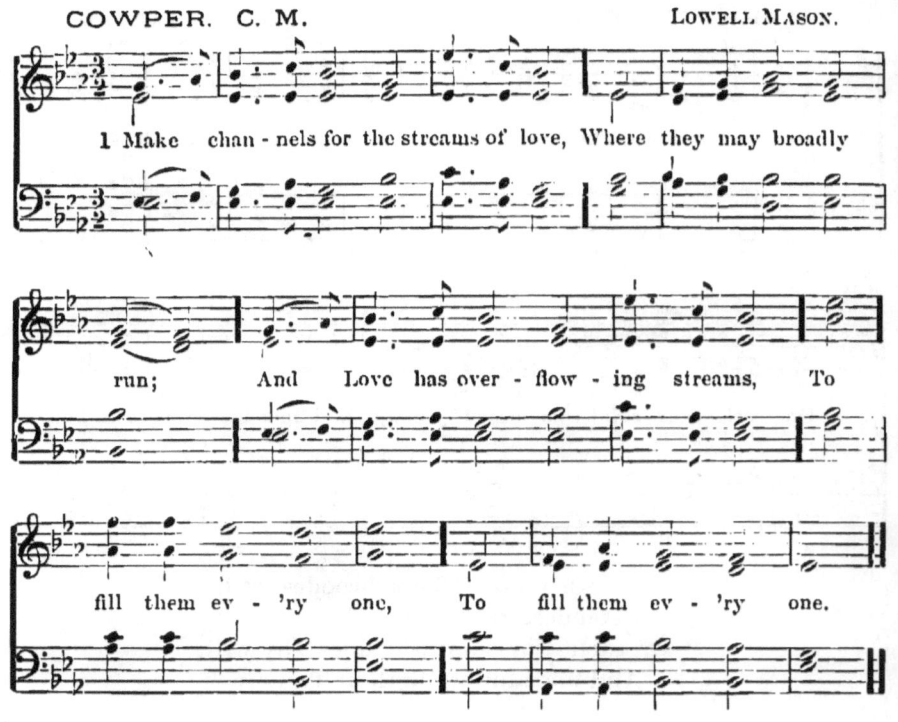

1 Make channels for the streams of love, Where they may broadly run; And Love has over-flowing streams, To fill them ev-'ry one, To fill them ev-'ry one.

1 Make channels for the streams of love,
   Where they may broadly run;
And Love has over-flowing streams,
   To fill them every one.

2 But if, at any time, we cease
   Such channels to provide,
The very founts of love for us
   Will soon be parched and dried.

3 For we must share, if we would keep
   That blessing from above;
Ceasing to give, we cease to have;
   Such is the law of love.
                         FRENCH.

LOVE. 93

LOVE DIVINE. 8, 7, D.   JOHN ZUNDEL.

1 Love di-vine, all love ex-cell-ing, Joy of heav'n, to earth come down!
Fix in us Thy hum-ble dwell-ing; All Thy faithful mer-cies crown.
D. S. Vis-it us with Thy sal-va-tion; En-ter ev-'ry trembling heart.
Je-sus, Thou art all com-pas-sion, Pure un-bounded love Thou art;

2 Breathe, O breathe Thy loving
    Spirit
Into every troubled breast!
Let us all in Thee inherit,
    Let us find that second rest.
Take away our bent to sinning;
    Alpha and Omega be;
End of faith, as its beginning,
    Set our hearts at liberty.

3 Come, almighty to deliver,
    Let us all Thy life receive;
Suddenly return, and never,
    Never more Thy temples
    leave:

Thee we would be always blessing,
    Serve Thee as Thy hosts above,
Pray, and praise Thee without
    ceasing,
Glory in Thy perfect love.

4 Finish then Thy new creation;
    Pure and spotless let us be;
Let us see Thy great salvation,
    Perfectly restored in Thee:
Changed from glory into glory,
    Till in heaven we take our place,
Till we cast our crowns before
    Thee,   [praise.
Lost, in wonder, love, and
                CHARLES WESLEY.

LOVE.

IN THE SILENT MIDNIGHT WATCHES. 8, 5.
H. P. Main.

1 Ev-'ry day hath toil and trouble, Ev-'ry heart hath care; Meek-ly bear thine own full measure, And thy brother's share; Fear not, shrink not, tho' the bur-den Heav-y to thee prove; God shall fill thy sense with gladness And thy heart with love.

2 Patiently enduring, ever
  Let thy spirit be,
Bound by links that cannot sever
  To Humanity,
Labor, wait! thy Master perished
  Ere His task was done;
Count not lost thy fleeting moments
  Life hath but begun.

3 Labor, wait! though midnight shadows,
  Gather round thee here,
And the storm above thee lowering
  Fill thy heart with fear:
Wait in hope! the morning dawneth
  When the night is gone,
And a peaceful rest awaits thee
  When thy work is done.
                BAILY.

LOVE.

EWING. 7, 6.   ALEXANDER EWING, 1861.

1 In heavenly love a-bid-ing, No change my heart shall fear; And safe is such con-fid-ing, For nothing changes here. The storm may rage without me, My hopes may low be laid, But God is round about me, I cannot be dismayed.

2 Wherever He may guide me,
   No want shall bring me back;
 My Shepherd is beside me,
   And nothing shall I lack.
 His wisdom ever waketh,
   His sight is never dim;
 He knows the path He taketh,
   And I will walk with Him.

3 Green pastures are before me,
   Which yet I have not seen;
 Bright skies will soon be o'er me,
   Where darkest clouds have been
 My hope I cannot measure,
   My path in life is free;
 My Father has my treasure,
   And He will walk with me.
                    ANNA L. WARING.

LOVE.

EVAN. C. M.   WM. H. HAVERGAL.

1 Who is thy neighbor? He whom thou
    Hast power to aid or bless;
  Whose aching heart or burning brow
    Thy soothing hand may press.

2 Thy neighbor? 'Tis the fainting poor,
    Whose eye with want is dim;
  O enter thou his humble door,
    With aid and peace for him.

3 Thy neighbor? He who drinks the cup
    When sorrow drowns the brim;
  With words of high, sustaining hope,
    Go thou and comfort him.
                  WM. B. O. PEABODY.

SERENITY. C. M.

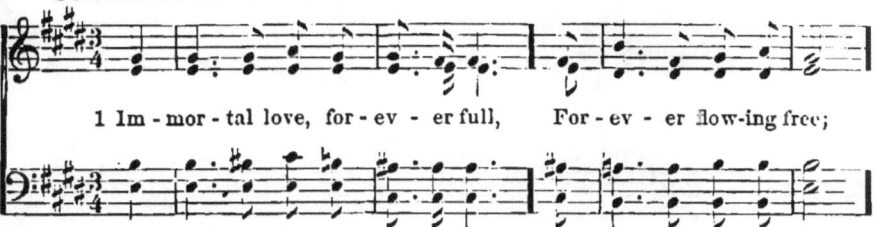

1 Im - mor - tal love, for - ev - er full, For - ev - er flow-ing free;

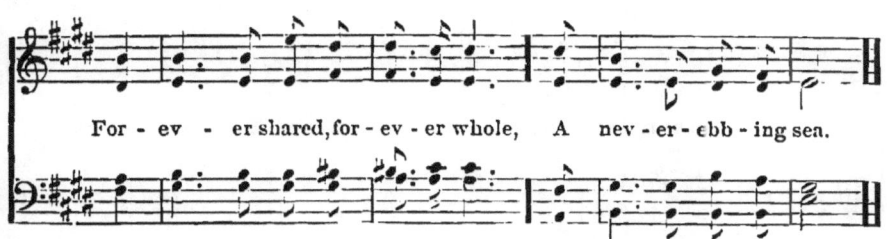

For - ev - er shared, for - ev - er whole, A nev - er - ebb - ing sea.

1 Immortal love forever full,
   Forever flowing free,
Forever shared, forever whole,
   A never-ebbing sea.

2 Our outward lips confess the name,
   All other names above;
But love alone knows whence it came,
   And comprehendeth love.

3 Blow, winds of God, awake and blow
   The mists of earth away;
Shine out, O Light divine, and show
   How wide and far we stray.

4 The letter fails, the systems fall
   And every symbol wanes;
The Spirit over-brooding all,
   Eternal Love remains.
              JOHN G. WHITTIER.

INNOCENTS. 7.   THIBAUT, 1254.

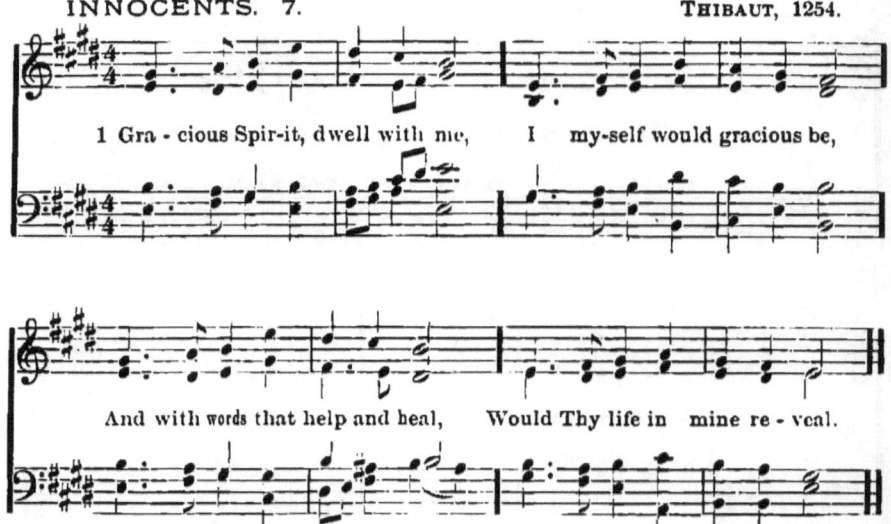

1 Gracious Spirit, dwell with me,
I myself would gracious be,
And with words that help and heal,
Would Thy life in mine reveal.

2 Truthful Spirit, dwell with me,
I myself would truthful be,
And Thy wisdom kind and clear
Let Thy life in mine appear.

3 Mighty Spirit, dwell with me,
I myself would mighty be;
Mighty so as to prevail,
Where unaided man must fail

4 Holy Spirit, dwell with me,
I myself would holy be,
Separate from sin, I would
Choose and cherish all things good.

5 Let my actions, brave and meek,
Christ's own gracious Spirit, speak,
Ever let this glorious hope
Press me on and bear me up.

                          THOS. L. LYNCH, 1855.

PRAYER.

ONTARIO. S. M.

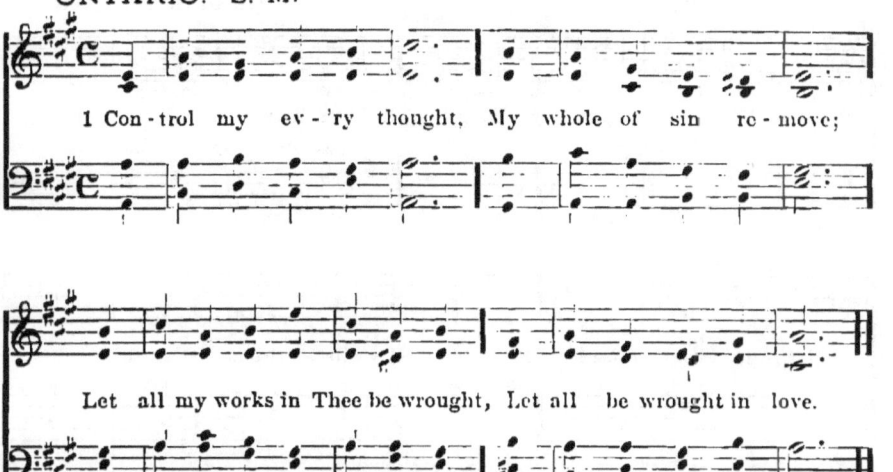

1 Control my every thought,
    My whole of sin remove;
  Let all my works in Thee be wrought,
    Let all be wrought in love.

2 O arm me with the mind,
    Meek Lamb, that was in Thee;
  And let my knowing zeal be joined
    With perfect charity.

3 O may I love like Thee!
    In all Thy footsteps tread;
  Thou hatest all uniquity,
    But nothing Thou hast made.

4 O may I learn the art
    With meekness to reprove;
  To hate the sin with all my heart,
    But still the sinner love.
                          CHARLES WESLEY.

PRAYER.

ITALY. 6, 4. FELICE GIARDINI, 1760.

1 Come, Thou al-might-y King! Help us Thy name to sing, Help us to praise! Fa-ther all-glo-ri-ous, O'er all vic-to-ri-ous, Come, and reign o-ver us, An-cient of days!

2 Come, Thou all-gracious God,
By heaven and earth adored,
Our prayer attend!
Come, and Thy children bless;
Give Thy word sure success;
Let Thine own holiness
On us descend.

3 Thou, Who did'st come to bring,
On Thy redeeming wing,
Healing and sight!
Health to the sick in mind,
Light to the inly blind,
Oh, now to all mankind
Let there be light!
WESLEY, 1757.

PRAYER.   101

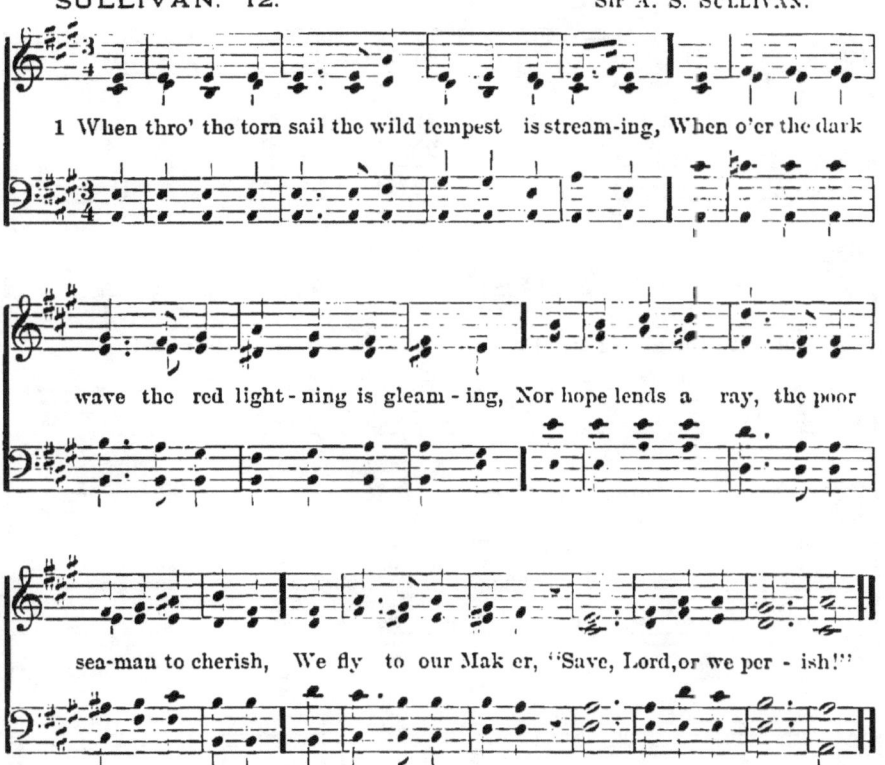

2 O Jesus, once tossed on the breast of the billow,
  Aroused by the shriek of despair from Thy pillow,
  Now seated in glory, the mariner cherish,
  Who cries in his anguish "Save, Lord, or we perish!"

3 And, Oh, when the whirlwind of passion is raging,
  When sin in our hearts its wild warfare is waging,
  Arise in Thy strength Thy redeemed to cherish;
  Rebuke the destroyer, "Save, Lord, or we perish!"
                                    REGINALD HEBER.

2 Implant it deep within,
  Whence it may ne'er remove,
The law of liberty from sin,
  The perfect law of love;
Thy nature be my law,
  My spotless sanctity
And sweetly every moment **draw**
  My happy soul to Thee.

2 Lord, my times are in Thy hand;
All my sanguine hopes have planned
To Thy wisdom I resign,
And would mould my will to Thine.
Thou my daily task shalt give;
Day by day to Thee I live;
So shall added years fulfill
Not my own, my Father's will.
             JOSIAH CONDER.

PRAYER.

ELEN. 7. Harmonized by CHAS. BEECHER.

1 Jesus, Lord, we look to Thee;
We will in Thy name agree;
Thou o'er us, the Prince of Peace;
Bid our jars for-ev-er cease;
By Thy reconciling love,
Ev-'ry stumbling-block remove.

2 Make us of one heart and mind,
Courteous, pitiful, and kind;
Lowly, meek, in thought and word,
Altogether like our Lord:
To Thy church the pattern give;
Show how true believers live.

3 Let us for each other care;
Each the other's burden bear;
Free from anger and from pride,
We will thus in God abide;
All the depths of love express,
All the heights of holiness.
CHAS. WESLEY.

PRAYER. 105

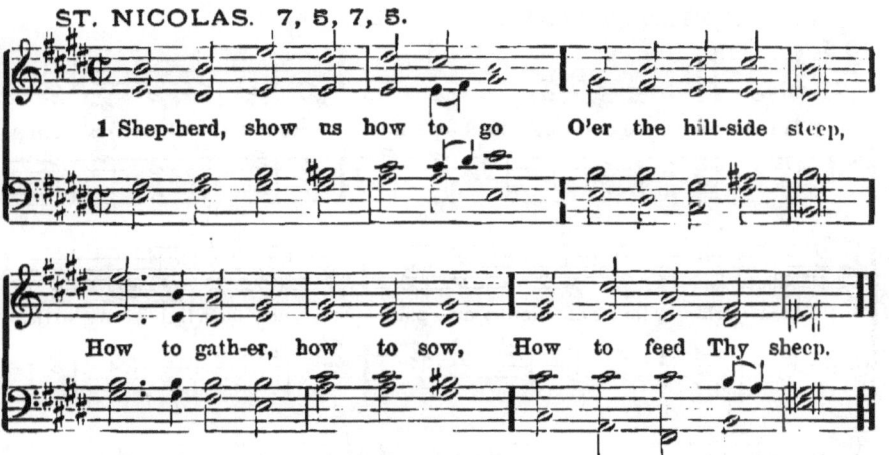

ST. NICOLAS. 7, 5, 7, 5.

1 Shepherd, show us how to go
O'er the hill-side steep,
How to gather, how to sow,
How to feed Thy sheep.

2 We will listen for Thy voice,
Lest our footsteps stray;
We will follow and rejoice,
All the rugged way.

3 Thou wilt bind the stubborn will,
Wound the callous breast,
Make self-righteousness be still,
Break earth's stupid rest.

4 Strangers on a barren shore,
Laboring long and lone—
We would enter by the door,
And Thou know'st Thine own.

5 So when day grows dark and cold,
Fear or triumph's harms,
Lead Thy lambkins to the fold,
Take us in Thine arms.

6 Feed the hungry, heal the heart,
Till the morning's beam;
White as wool, ere we depart—
Shepherd, wash us clean.

Rev. MARY B. G. EDDY.

106   PRAYER.

THE ROSEATE HUES. C. M. D.

1 What time the ev-'ning shad-ows fall A-round the Church on earth,
When dark-er forms of doubt ap-pal, And new false lights have birth:
'hen clos-er should her faith-ful band, For truth to-geth-er hold,
Hell's last de-vic-es to with-stand. And safe-ly guard her fold.

2 O Christ, Who for Thy flock didst
   That all might be as one. [pray.
  Unite us all ere fades the day,
   Thou Sole-Begotten Son;
  The East, the West, together bind
   In love's unbroken chain ;
  Give each one hope, one heart one
   One glory and one gain. [mind,

3 O Spirit, Lord of light and life,
   The Church with strength renew,
  Compose the angry voice of strife,
   All jealousies subdue :

Do Thou in ever-quickening streams
   Upon Thy saints descend,
And warm them with reviving beams
   And guide them to the end.

4 Great Three in One, great One in Three,
   Our hymns of prayer receive,
  And teach us all from sin to flee,
   And live as we believe; [speech
  So, pure in faith, our thoughts and
   And acts that faith, shall own ;
  So shall we Thy presence reach,
   And know as we are known.

PRAYER.

FAITHFUL SHEPHERD. 6, 5.
L. J. Hutton.

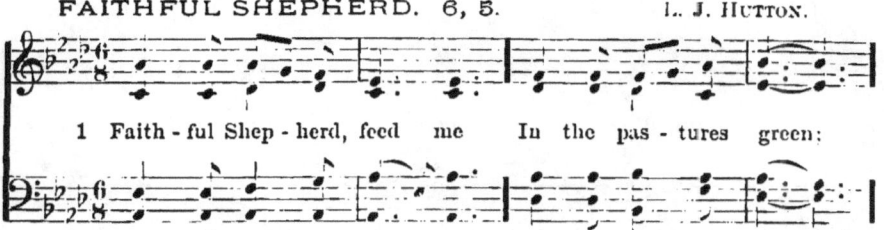

1 Faithful Shepherd, feed me In the pastures green:

Faithful Shepherd, lead me Where Thy steps are seen.

1 Faithful Shepherd, feed me
  In the pastures green;
  Faithful Shepherd, lead me
  Where Thy steps are seen.

2 Hold me fast, and guide me
  In the narrow way;
  So with Thee beside me,
  I shall never stray.

3 Hallow every pleasure,
  Every gift and pain;
  Be Thyself my treasure,
  Though none else I gain.

4 Day by day prepare me
  As Thou seest best;
  Then let angels bear me
  To Thy promised rest.
         Rev. T. B. Pollock, abr.

108   PRAYER.

1 O grant, dear Lord, this prayer to me,
   That I may know the Truth in Thee;
   Onward through night, I seek the way,
   Guide Thou my steps to perfect day.

2 O may I know, that I am Thine,
   Thine own pure thought, O Truth Divine,
   Thy Light, Thy Love shall conquer strife,
   And give me peace in Thee, my Life.
                       F. A. F.

PRAYER.   109

OLMUTZ. S. M.   Arr. by Dr. MASON.

1 Teach us Thy way, O God; Thine is a pleasant way;
Through pastures green, by waters still Our feet would gladly stray.

1 Teach us Thy way, O God;
    Thine is a pleasant way,
  Through pastures green, by waters still
    Our feet would gladly stray.

2 Thine is a living way,
    In death it has no part;
  From fear of all disease and sin
    It will relieve the heart.

3 The Spirit's sweet control,
    Freely we will confess;
  Fly to Thine outstretched arms of love,
    And there find health and rest.

4 No ravenous beast is there;
    Thy way gives blest release
  From every raging, savage foe;
    Its name is Holiness.

M. J. H. ZINK.

110 PRAYER.

WARD. L. M.   Scotch Melody, Arr. by Dr. MASON.

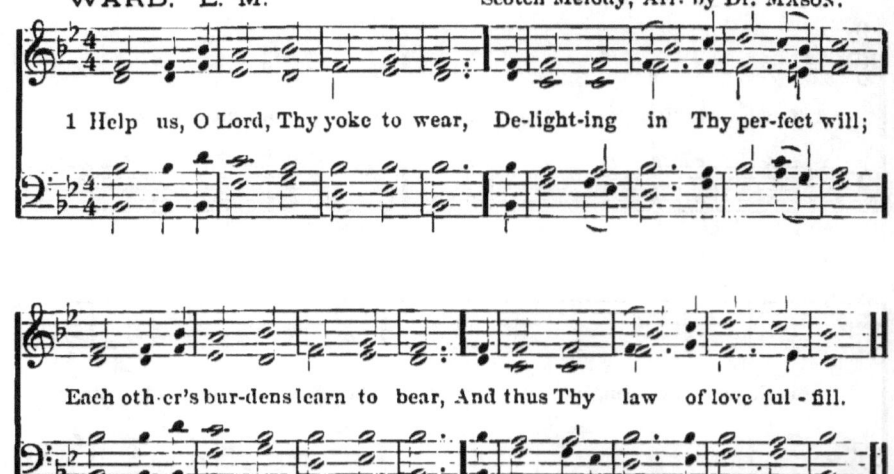

1 Help us, O Lord, Thy yoke to wear, De-light-ing in Thy per-fect will;
Each oth-er's bur-dens learn to bear, And thus Thy law of love ful - fill.

    1 Help us, O Lord, Thy yoke to wear,
        Delighting in Thy perfect will;
    Each other's burdens learn to bear,
        And thus Thy law of love fulfill.

    2 He that hath pity on the poor
        Lendeth his substance to the Lord;
    And, lo! his recompense is sure,
        For more than all shall be restored.

    3 Teach us, with glad, ungrudging heart,
        As Thou hast blest our various store,
    From our abundance to impart
        A liberal portion to the poor.

    4 To Thee, our all devoted be,
        In whom we breathe, and move, and **live**:
    Freely we have received from Thee;
        Freely may we rejoice to give.
                THOMAS COTTERILL.

PRAYER. **111**

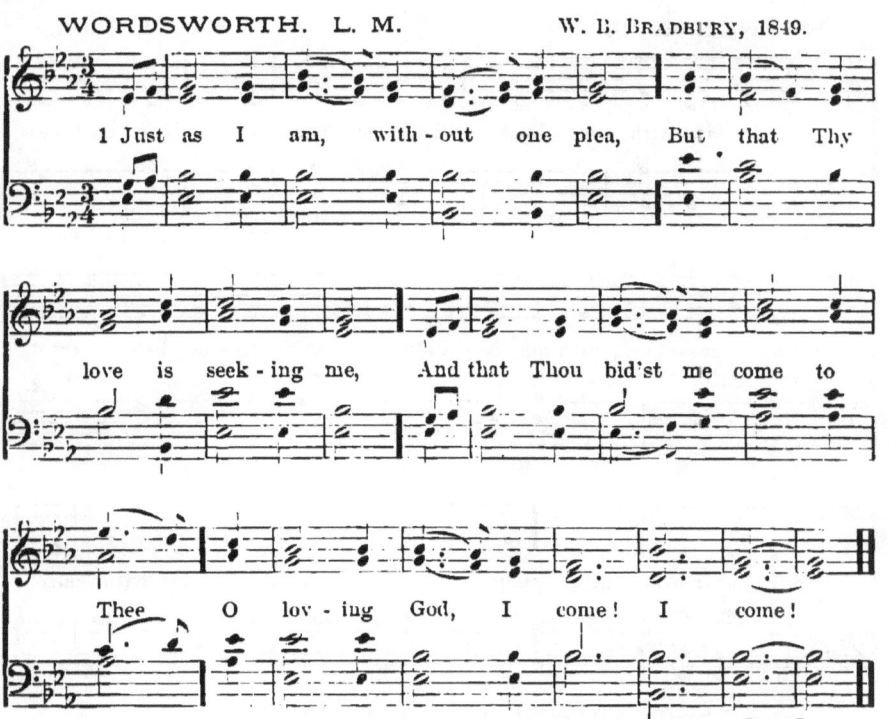

WORDSWORTH. L. M.   W. B. BRADBURY, 1849.

1 Just as I am, without one plea,
  But that Thy love is seeking me,
  And that Thou bid'st me come to Thee,
  O loving God, I come! I come!

2 Just as I am, though tossed about
  With many a conflict, many a doubt,
  Fightings within, and fears without,
  O loving God, I come! I come!

3 Just as I am, Thou wilt receive,
  Wilt welcome, pardon, heal, relieve;
  Because Thy promise I believe,
  O loving God, I come! I come!
Hymns of the Spirit.

112 PRAYER.

EVENTIDE. 10. WM. H. MONK.

2 Swift to its close ebbs out life's little day;
  Earth's joys grow dim, its glories pass away;
  Change and decay in all around I see;
  O Thou, who changest not, abide with me!

3 I need Thy presence every passing hour;
  What but Thy love can foil the tempter's power?
  Who, like Thyself, my guide and stay can be?
  Through cloud and sunshine, Lord, abide with me!

4 I fear no foe, with Thee at hand to bless;
  Ills have no weight, and tears no bitterness;
  Where is death's sting? where, grave, thy victory?
  I triumph still if Thou abide with me.

5 Hold Thou Thy cross before my closing eyes;
  Shine through the gloom and point me to the skies;
  Heaven's morning breaks, and earth's vain shadows flee;
  Death lost in life, my Lord, abides with me!
  HENRY F. LYTE.

HEALING. 113

ROUSSEAU. L. M.   Rousseau.

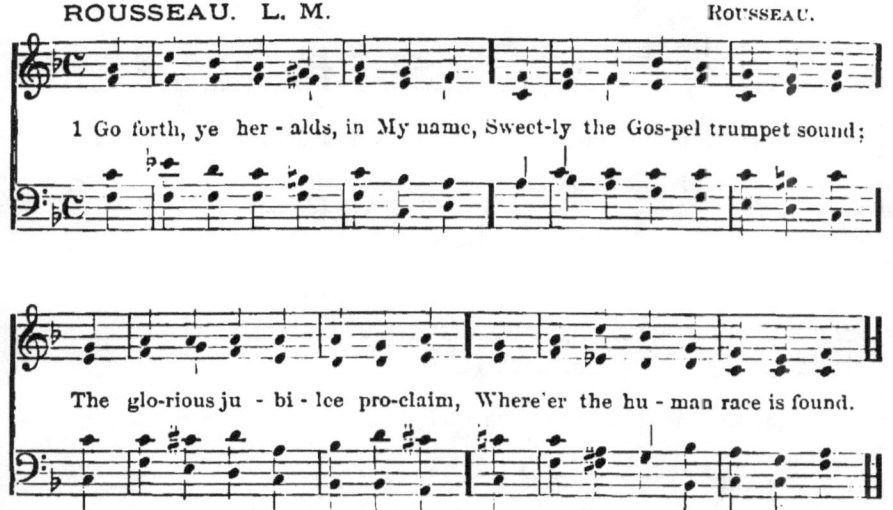

1 Go forth, ye heralds, in My name,
   Sweetly the Gospel trumpet sound;
  The glorious jubilee proclaim,
   Where'er the human race is found.

2 The joyful news to all impart,
   And teach them where salvation lies;
  With care bind up the broken heart,
   And wipe the tears from weeeping eyes.

3 Be wise as serpents, where you go,
   But harmless as a peaceful dove;
  And let your heaven-taught conduct show
   Ye are commissioned from above.

4 Freely from Me, ye have received,
   Freely, in love, to others give;
  Thus shall your doctrines be believed,
   And, by your labors, sinners live.
                        J. Logan.

HEALING.

ATHOL. S. M.   Ralph Harrison, 1786.

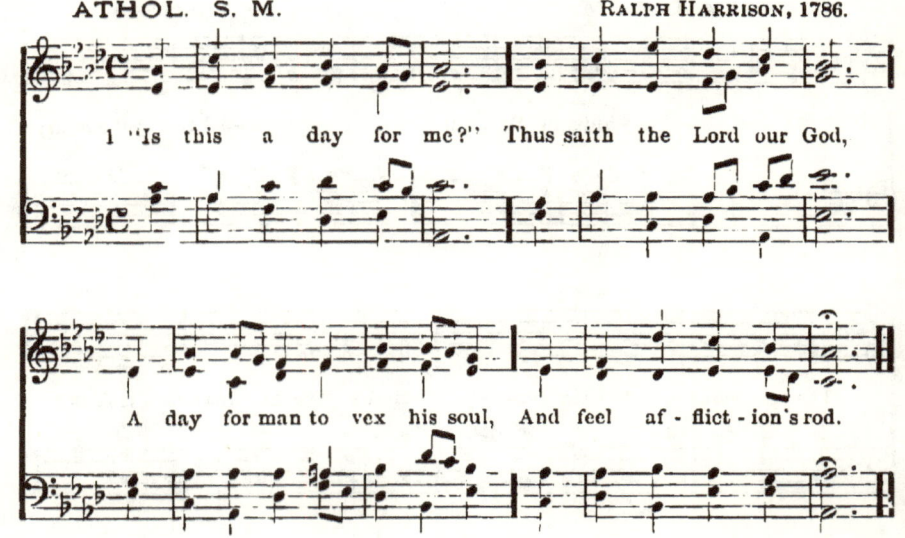

1 "Is this a day for me?"
   Thus saith the Lord our God,
A day for man to vex his soul,
   And feel affliction's rod.

2 No, is not this alone,
   The sacred fast I choose,
Oppression's yoke to burst in twain,
   The bonds of guilt to loose.

3 To nakedness and want
   Your food and raiment deal,
To dwell in harmony with all,
   And sin and sickness heal.

4 Then, like the morning ray,
   Shall spring your health and light;
Before you righteousness shall shine,
   Behind, My glory bright.
                  Drummond.

HEALING.

DWIGHT. L. M. Arr. by J. P. Holbrook.

1 When the blind suppliant in the way, By friendly hands to Jesus led, Prayed to behold the light of day, "Receive thy sight," the Savior said.

1 When the blind suppliant in the way,
   By friendly hands to Jesus led,
Prayed to behold the light of day,
   "Receive thy sight," the Savior said.

2 At once he saw the pleasant rays
   That lit the glorious firmament;
And, with firm step and words of praise,
   He followed where the Master went.

3 Look down in pity, Lord, we pray,
   On eyes oppressed by moral night,
And touch the darkened lids, and say
   The gracious words, "Receive thy sight."

4 Then, in clear daylight, shall we see
   Where walked the sinless Son of God;
And, aided by new strength from Thee,
   Press onward in the path He trod.
                        Wm. C. Bryant.

116 HEALING.

WHITTIER. 10.   Arr. from a Jewish Chant.

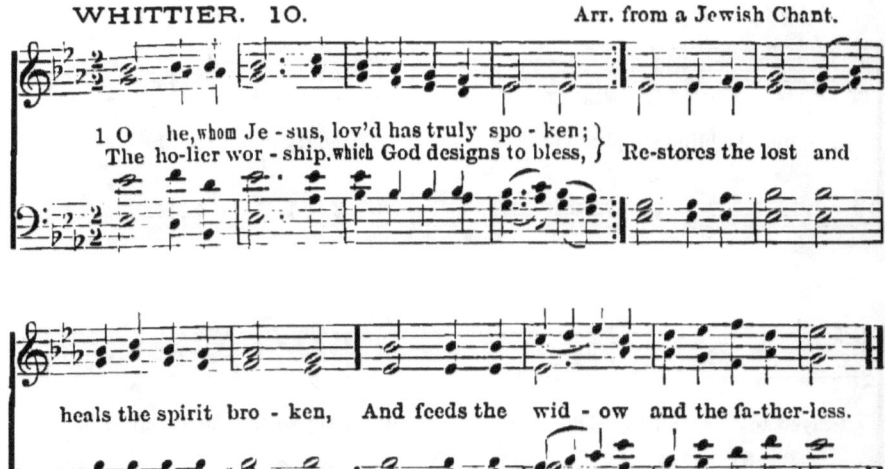

1 O he, whom Jesus lov'd has truly spo-ken;
The ho-lier wor-ship, which God designs to bless,
Re-stores the lost and heals the spirit bro-ken,
And feeds the wid-ow and the fa-ther-less.

1 O he, whom Jesus loved, has truly spoken,
    The holier worship, which God designs to bless,
Restores the lost and heals the spirit broken,
    And feeds the widow and the fatherless.

2 Then, brother-man, fold to thy heart thy brother;
    For where God dwells, the peace of God is there;
To worship rightly is to love each other,
    Each smile a hymn, and kindly deed a prayer.

3 Follow, with reverent steps, the great example
    Of Him, whose holy works was doing good;
So shall the wide earth seem our Father's temple,
    Each loving life a psalm of gratitude.

4 Thus shall all shackles fall, the stormy clangor
    Of wild war, music o'er the earth shall cease;
Love shall tread out the baleful fires of anger,
    And, in its ashes, plant the tree of peace.
                                    WHITTIER.

HEALING.

BRATTLE-STREET. C. M. D.   Ignace Pleyel, 1791.

1 Beneath the thick, but breaking cloud,
    We talk of Christian life;
  The words of Jesus on our lips,
    Our hearts with man at strife.
  Traditions, forms, and selfish aims,
    Have dimmed the inner light,
  Have closely veiled the spirit world.
    And angels from our sight.

2 Strong souls and willing hands we need,
    Our temple to repair,
  Remove the gathering dust of years,
    And show the model fair;
  We slumber while the present calls,
    And darkness grows with rest;
  Would'st see the truth? To actions wake,
    To do Divine behest.
                                    Anon.

118   HEALING.

REQUIEM. 8, 7, 8, 7, 7, 7.

1 Thou to Whom the sick and dying
Ever came, nor came in vain,
Still with healing word replying
To the wearied cry of pain,
Hear us, Savior, as we meet,
Suppliants at Thy mercy-seat.

2 Still the weary, sick, and dying
   Need a brother's, sister's care,
On Thy higher help relying
   May we now their burden share,
Bringing all our offerings meet
Suppliants at Thy mercy-seat.

3 May each child of Thine be willing,
   Willing both in hand and heart,
At the law of love fulfilling,
   Ever comfort to impart;
Ever bringing offerings meet,
Suppliant to Thy mercy-seat.

4 So may sickness, sin, and sadness
   To Thy healing virtue yield;
Till the sick and sad, in gladness,
   Rescued, ransomed, cleansed, healed,
One in Thee together meet
Pardon at Thy judgement-seat.

MENDON. L. M.   Arr. by L. MASON.

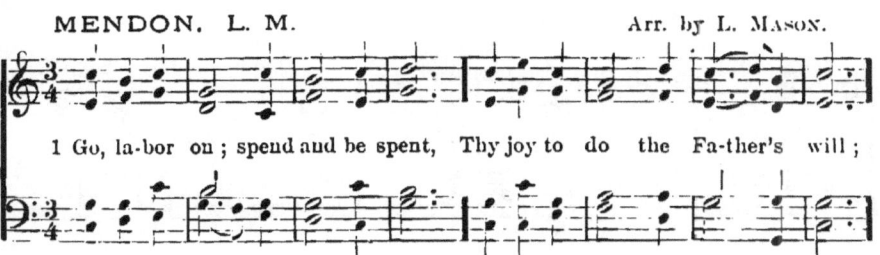

1 Go, labor on; spend and be spent, Thy joy to do the Father's will;

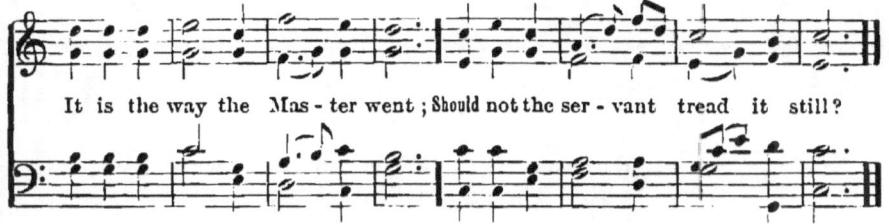

It is the way the Master went; Should not the servant tread it still?

2 Go, labor on; 'tis not for naught;
   Thine earthly loss is heavenly gain;
   Men heed Thee, love Thee, praise Thee not;
   The Master praises—what are men?

3 Go, labor on; your hands are weak;
   Your knees are faint, your soul cast down;
   Yet falter not; the prize you seek
   Is near—a kingdom and a crown!

4 Toil on, faint not; keep watch, and pray!
   Be wise the erring soul to win;
   Go forth into the world's highway;
   Compel the wanderer to come in.

5 Toil on, and in thy toil rejoice;
   For toil comes rest, for exile home;
   Soon shalt thou hear the Bridegroom's voice,
   The midnight peal, "Behold, I come!"
                                  HORATIUS BONAR.

HEALING.

ST. TIMOTHY. C. M.

1 O Tender One, O Mighty One,
  Who never sent away
  The sinner or the sufferer,
  Thou art the same to-day.

2 The same in Love, the same in Power,
  And Thou art waiting, still,
  To heal the multitudes that come,
  Yea, "whosoever will."

3 We know Thee, blessed Savior,
  Who hast "filled us with good things;"
  Thou hast risen in our land,
  With healing in Thy wings.

4 Thou hast risen on our hearts,
  With light and life divine;
  Now bid us be Thy messengers,
  Bid us "Arise and shine."

5 Oh, let Thy Spirit fire our zeal,
  That we may now "send out,"
  And tell that Thou art come
  "In all the country round about."

6 That Thou art waiting now to heal,
  That Thou art strong to save,
  That Thou hast spoilt the spoiler, Death,
  And triumphed o'er the grave.
                      FRANCES R. HAVERGAL.

HEALING.

ST. OSWALD. 8, 7.

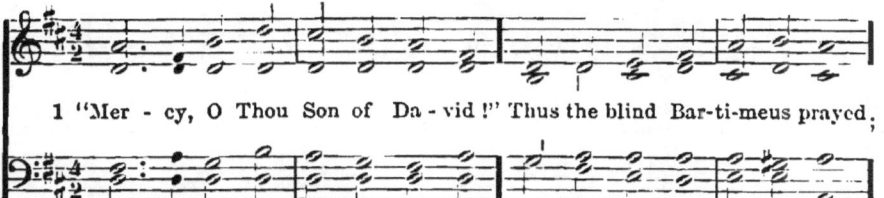

1 "Mer - cy, O Thou Son of Da - vid !" Thus the blind Bar-ti-meus prayed;

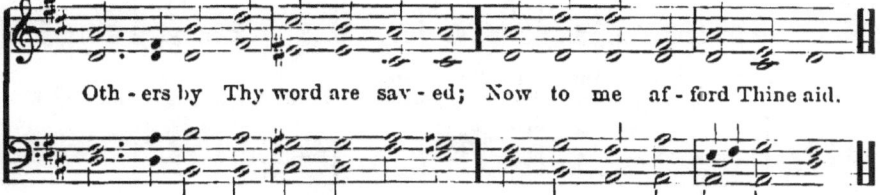

Oth - ers by Thy word are sav - ed; Now to me af - ford Thine aid.

2 Many for his crying, chid him,
   But he called the louder still,
Till the gracious Savior bid him,
   Come and ask Me what you will.

3 Money was not what he wanted,
   Though by begging used to live;
But he asked, and Jesus granted
   Alms which none but He could give,

5 Lord, remove this grievous blindness,
   Let my eyes behold the day;
Straight he saw and, won by kindness,
   Followed Jesus in the way.

5 Oh! that all the blind but knew Him.
   And would be advised by me;
Surely they would hasten to Him,
   He would cause them all to see.
                  NEWTON.

122 HEALING.

YOAKLEY. L. M. 61.   Rev. W. YOAKLEY.

1 Around Bethesda's healing bower,
   Waiting to hear the rustling wing;
Which, spoke the angel nigh, whose power
   Gave virtue to that holy spring;
With patience and with hope endued,
   Were seen the gathering multitude.

2 Had they who watched and waited there,
   Been conscious of the healing thought,
With what unceasing, anxious care
   Would they that quickening flood have sought,
And with what fervency of soul,
   The power divine to make them whole.
                                  Unknown.

HEALING. 123

ST. MATTHEW. D. C. M.

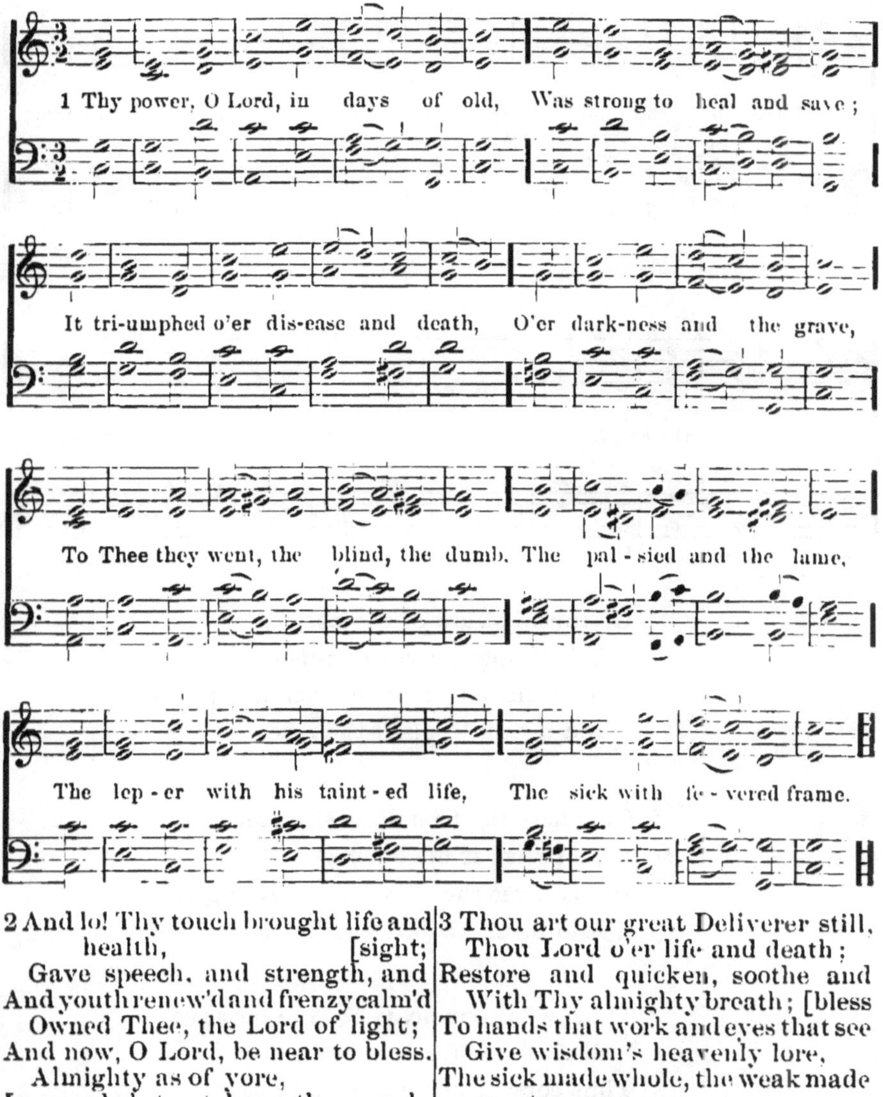

1 Thy power, O Lord, in days of old, Was strong to heal and save;
It triumphed o'er disease and death, O'er darkness and the grave,
To Thee they went, the blind, the dumb, The palsied and the lame,
The leper with his tainted life, The sick with fevered frame.

2 And lo! Thy touch brought life and health, [sight;
Gave speech, and strength, and sight;
And youth renew'd and frenzy calm'd
Owned Thee, the Lord of light;
And now, O Lord, be near to bless.
Almighty as of yore,
In crowded street, by restless couch,
As by Gennesareth's shore.

3 Thou art our great Deliverer still,
Thou Lord o'er life and death;
Restore and quicken, soothe and bless
With Thy almighty breath; [bless
To hands that work and eyes that see
Give wisdom's heavenly lore,
The sick made whole, the weak made strong,
May praise Thee evermore.

HEALING.

HOLY CROSS. C. M.   MENDELSSOHN.

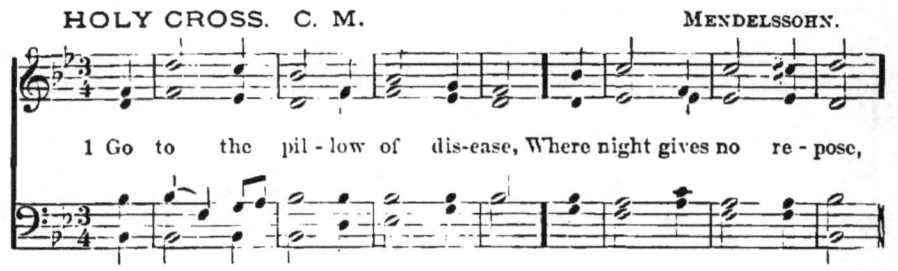

1 Go to the pillow of disease, Where night gives no repose,

And on the cheek where sickness preys, Bid health to plant the rose.

1 Go to the pillow of disease,
   Where night gives no repose,
And on the cheek where sickness preys,
   Bid health to plant the rose.

2 Go where the friendless stranger lies,
   To perish is his doom;
Snatch from the grave his closing eyes,
   And bring his blessing home.

3 Thus, what our heavenly Father gave
   Shall we as freely give;
Thus copy Him, who lived to save,
   And teach us how to live.

TOPLADY. 7, 61
THOS. HASTINGS.

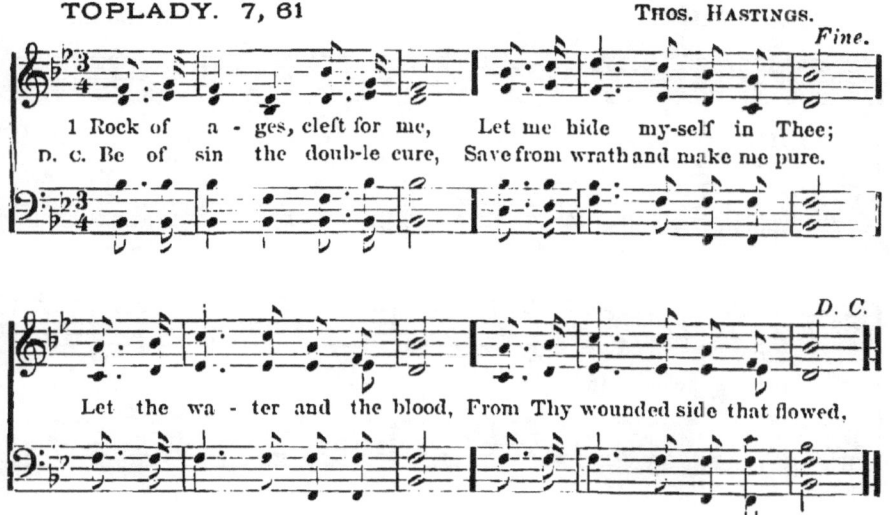

1 Rock of a-ges, cleft for me, Let me hide my-self in Thee;
D. C. Be of sin the double cure, Save from wrath and make me pure.

Let the wa-ter and the blood, From Thy wounded side that flowed.

1 Rock of Ages, cleft for me,
Let me hide myself in Thee;
Let the water and the blood,
From Thy wounded side that flowed,
Be of sin the double cure,
Save from wrath and make me pure.

2 Could my tears forever flow,
Could my zeal no languor know,
These for sin could not atone;
Thou must save, and Thou alone:
In my hand no price I bring;
Simply to Thy cross I cling.

3 While I draw this fleeting breath,
When my eyes shall close in death
When I rise to worlds unknown,
And behold Thee on Thy throne
Rock of Ages, cleft for me,
Let me hide myself in Thee.

AUGUSTUS M. TOPLADY, alt

GRATITUDE. L. M. Rev. Ami Bost, Arr. by T. Hastings.

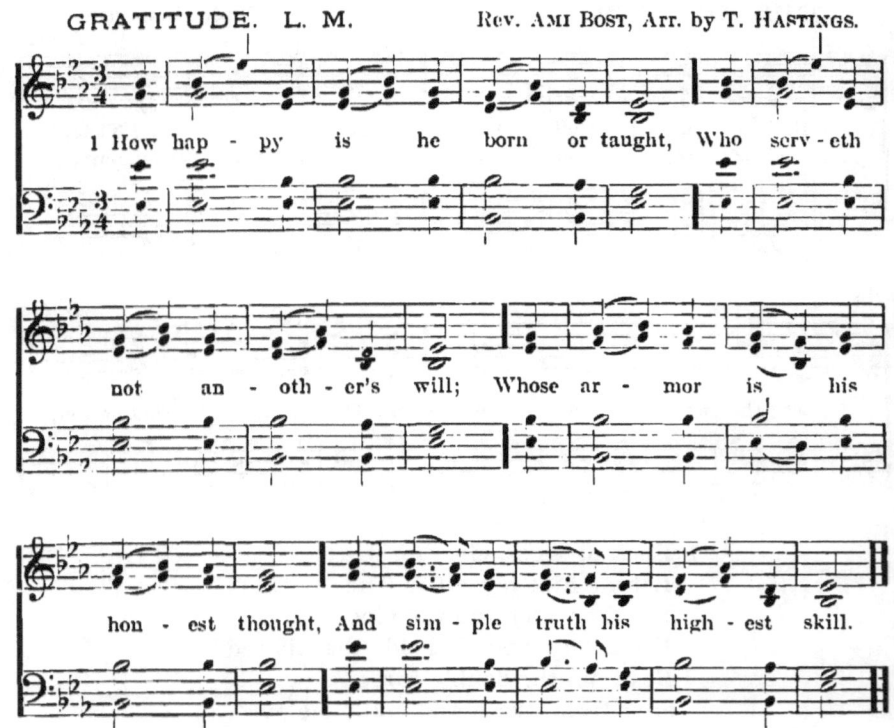

1 How happy is he born or taught,
  Who serveth not another's will;
  Whose armor is his honest thought,
  And simple truth his highest skill.

2 Who God doth late and early pray
  More of His grace than goods to lend;
  And walks with man, from day to day,
  As with a brother and a friend.

3 This man is freed from servile bands
  Of hope to rise, or fear to fall;
  Lord of himself and not of lands,
  And having nothing, yet hath all.
  Sir. Henry Wotton.

MARRION. P. M.   From MENDELSSOHN by MARRION SMITH. C. S.

1 Thy kingdom here, Lord, can it be? Searching and seeking ev'rywhere, For many a year, "Thy Kingdom come" has been my prayer; Was that dear kingdom all the while so near?

2 Blinded and dull
   With selfish sin,
  Have I been sitting at the gate,
   Called Beautiful,
  Where Thy fair angel stands and waits
   With hand upon the lock to let me in.

3 Was I the wall,
   Which barred the way,
  Darkening the glory of Thy grace,
   Hiding the ray,
  Which, shining out as from Thy face
   Had shown to other men the perfect day?

4 Let me not sit,
   Another hour
  Waiting, what is mine all to win
   Blinded in wit;
  Lord Jesus, rend these walls of sin,
  Beat down the gate that I may enter it.
                        SUSAN COOLIDGE.

WEBB. 7, 6. G. J. WEBB.

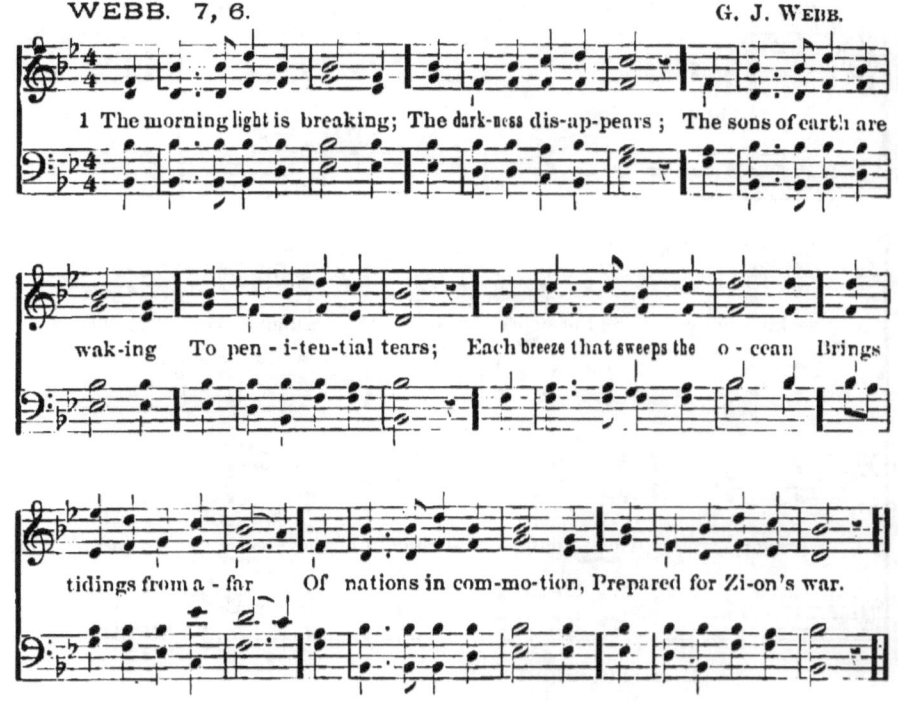

1 The morning light is breaking; The darkness disappears; The sons of earth are waking To penitential tears; Each breeze that sweeps the ocean Brings tidings from afar Of nations in commotion, Prepared for Zion's war.

2 Rich dews of grace come o'er us
 In many a gentle shower,
And brighter scenes before us
 Are opening every hour;
Each prayer to heaven going,
 Abundant answers brings,
And heavenly gales are blowing,
 With peace upon their wings.

3 Blest river of salvation,
 Pursue thy onward way;
Flow thou to every nation,
 Nor in thy richness stay;
Stay not till all the lowly
 Triumphant reach their home;
Stay not till all the holy
 Proclaim, "The Lord is come."
  S. F. SMITH.

ST. CECILIA. L. M.

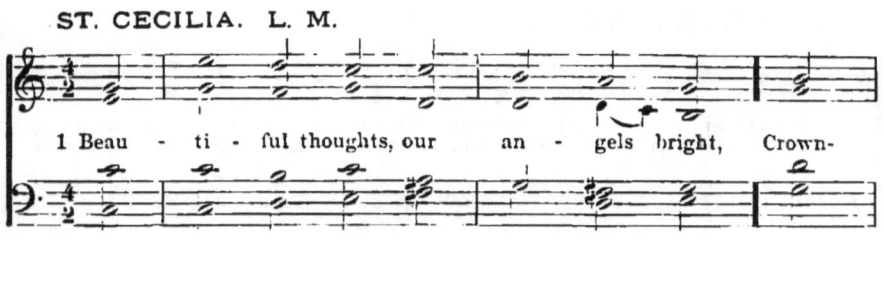

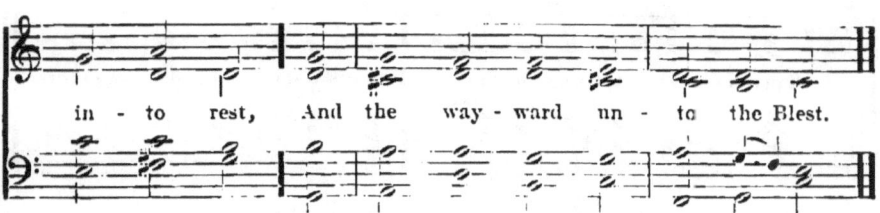

1 Beautiful thoughts, our angels bright,
Crowned with Love's most glorious light,
Lifting the weary into rest,
And the wayward unto the Blest.

2 Beautiful thoughts, our angels fair,
Shining to brighten, bless, and cheer,
Lighting us upward to the light,
Bringing morning after the night.

3 Beautiful thoughts are angels here,
Gifts of the Spirit, priceless, dear,
Stay with us ever, change this strife
To peace, to harmony and life.

GENERAL HYMNS.

MORNING STAR. 7,

1 Watchman, tell us of the night,
    What its signs of promise are.
  Traveler, o'er yon mountain's height,
    See that glory-beaming star!
  Watchman, does its beauteous ray
    Aught of hope or joy foretell?
  Traveler, yes; it brings the day,
    Promised day of Israel.

2 Watchman, tell us of the night!
    Higher yet that star ascends;
  Traveler, blessedness and light,
    Peace and truth, its course portends!
  Watchman, will its beams alone
    Gild the spot that gave them birth?
  Traveler, ages are its own.
    Lo! it bursts o'er all the earth!

3 Watchman, tell us of the night,
    For the morning seems to dawn!
  Traveler, darkness takes its flight;
    Doubt and terror are withdrawn.
  Watchman, let thy wandering cease;
    Hie thee to thy quiet home!
  For behold! the Prince of peace,
    Lo! the Son of God is come!
                        BOWRING.

RATHBUN. 8, 7.   ITHAMAR CONKEY, 1851.

1 Father, hast Thou not a message,
   To be born in melody,
   To the hearts of suffering thousands;
   Unsustained by hopes of Thee?

2 Low down in each heart are longings,
   That to song, responsive spring;
   Songs of heaven, I long to sing them,
   That they may with gladness ring.

3 Lord, Thou didst inspire the prophets,
   I would follow and serve Thee;
   Patiently I listen! might not
   Seraphs whisper them to me?

PEARSALL. 7, 6, D. L. TUTTIETT.

1 Go forward, Christian soldier, Beneath thy Leader true:
The Lord Himself thy Captain, Does all thy foes subdue.
His love foretells thy trials, He knows thine hourly need;
He can, with bread of heaven, Thy fainting spirit feed.

2 Go forward, Christian soldier,
　Nor dream of peaceful rest,
Till Satan's hosts are vanquished,
　And harmony possessed;
Till God Himself shall call thee
　To lay thy armor by,
And wear, in endless glory,
　The crown of victory.

3 Go forward, Christian soldier,
　Fear not the gathering night,
The Lord has been thy shelter.
　The Lord will be thy Light:
When morn, His face revealeth,
　Thy dangers all are past;
And nought His love concealeth,
　It holds thee to the last.

　　　　　L. TUTTIETT.

BOARDMAN. C. M.   DEVEREUX, Arr. by G. KINGSLEY, 1853.

1 We bless Thee for Thy peace, O God,
   Deep as the soundless sea
Which falls like sunshine all abroad
   On those who trust in Thee.

2 We ask not, Father, for repose,
   That comes from outward rest,
If we may have through all life's woes
   Thy peace within our breast.

3 A peace that flows serene and deep,
   A river in the soul,
Whose banks a living verdure keep,
   God's sunshine o'er the whole.
NORCROSS.

STATE STREET. S. M.   J. C. WOODMAN.

1 Teach me on Thee to wait,
   Till I can all things do,
On Thee, Almighty to create
   Almighty to renew.

2 I rest upon Thy word;
   The promise is for me;
My succor and salvation, Lord,
   Shall surely come from Thee.

3 If done beneath Thy laws,
   E'en servile labors shine;
Hallowed is toil, if this the cause,
   The meanest work divine.
                     GEORGE HERBERT.

HANOVER. 11, 10.   J. C. W. A. MOZART.

1 Hail to the brightness of Zion's glad morning! Joy to the lands that in darkness have lain! Hushed be the accents of sorrow and mourning; Zion in triumph begins her mild reign.

2 Hail to the brightness of Zion's glad morning,
   Long by the prophets of Israel foretold;
   Hail to the millions from bondage returning;
   Gentiles and Jews the blest vision behold.

3 Lo, in the desert rich flowers are springing;
   Streams ever copious are gliding along;
   Loud from the mountain-tops echoes are ringing;
   Wastes rise in verdure, and mingle in song.

4 See, from all lands, from the isles of the ocean,
   Praise to Jehovah ascending on high;
   Fallen are the engines of war and commotion
   Shouts of salvation are rending the sky.
                                    THOS. HASTINGS.

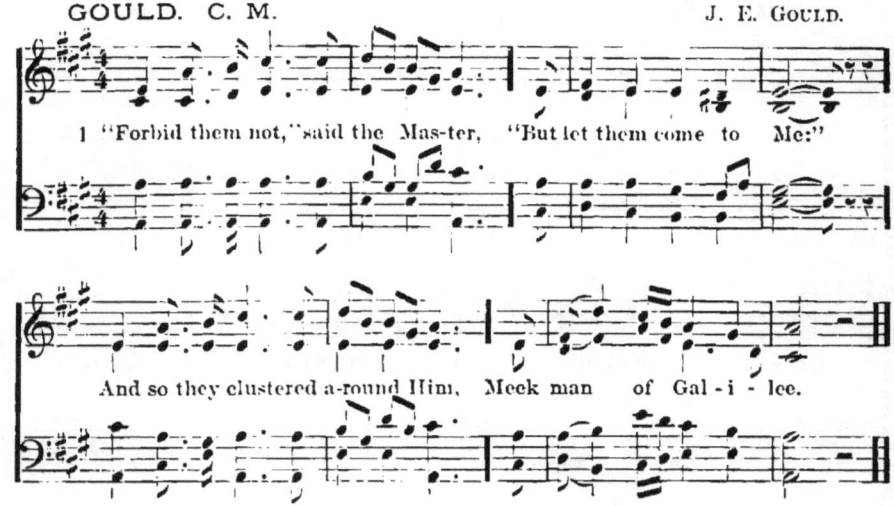

2 They missed not the pomp and glory,
   To older hearts so dear;
For they caught the cadence of heaven,
   In tones so true and clear.

3 They saw the wonderful city,
   Whose streets were glistening gold;
For they saw the beatific vision
   Of shepherd, flock and fold.

4 He gathered them in His bosom
   Safe from sorrow and sin,
Into that heavenly kingdom,
   And discords come not in.

5 Again Christ's Spirit is brooding,
   Over our weary world,
The banners of peace are flying,
   Not again to be furled.

6 And again the little children,
   Loving and pure and young,
Are singing the grand old anthem,
   The stars of morning sung.

             JOSEPHINE C. WOODBURY.

ANGELS' SONG. 11, 10.   Rev. J. B. Dykes.

1. Still, still with thee, when purple morning breaketh,
When the bird waketh, and the shadows flee;
Fairer than morning, lovelier than the daylight,
Dawns the sweet consciousness, I am with thee.

2. So shall it be at last in that bright morning,
When the soul waketh and earth's shadows flee;
Oh, in that hour, fairer than daylight dawning,
Shall rise the glorious thought, I am with thee.

                                     Harriet B. Stowe.

REDHEAD. 8, 7, 8, 7.

1 Ho-ly brethren, called and chos-en, By the sovereign voice of might: See your high and ho-ly call-ing, Out of dark-ness in-to light.

2 Called according to His purpose,
   And the riches of His Love;
Won to listen, by the leading
   Of the gentle, Heavenly Dove,

3 Called to suffer with our Master,
   Patiently to run His race;
Called a blessing to inherit,
   Called to holiness and grace.

4 Called to fellowship with Jesus,
   By the Ever-faithful One;
Called to His eternal glory
   To the kingdom of His Son.

5 Whom He calleth, He preserveth,
   And His glory they shall see;
He is faithful that hath called you,
   He will do it, fear not ye.

6 Therefore, holy brethren, onward!
   Thus ye make your calling sure;
For the prize of this high calling,
   Bravely to the end endure.
                  FRANCES R. HAVERGAL.

MANOAH. C. M.   From F. J. HAYDN.

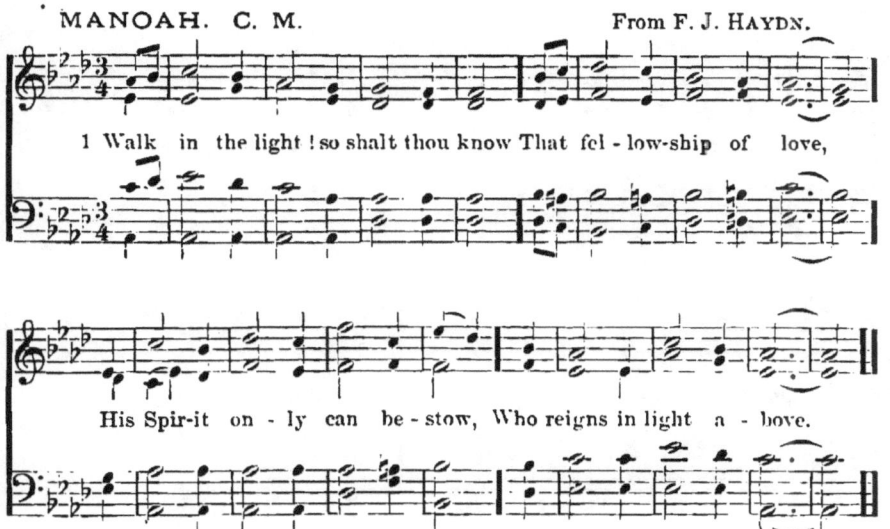

1 Walk in the light! so shalt thou know That fel-low-ship of love, His Spir-it on-ly can be-stow, Who reigns in light a-bove.

2 Walk in the light! and thou shalt find
   Thy heart made truly His,
Who dwells in cloudless light enshrined,
   In whom no darkness is.

3 Walk in the light! and thou shalt own
   Thy darkness passed away,
Because that light hath on thee shone
   In which is perfect day.

4 Walk in the light! and e'en the tomb
   No fearful shade shall wear;
Glory shall chase away its gloom,
   For Christ hath conquered there.

5 Walk in the light! thy path shall be
   Peaceful, serene, and bright:
For God, by grace, shall dwell in thee,
   And God Himself is light.
                  BERNARD BARTON.

140   GENERAL HYMNS.

EASTON. L. M.   Mozart.

1 The starry firmament on high,
And all the glories of the sky,
Yet shine not to Thy praise, O Lord,
So brightly as Thy written word.

2 The hopes that holy word supplies,
Its truths divine and precepts wise,
In each a heavenly beam I see,
And every beam conducts to Thee.

3 Almighty Lord, the sun shall fail,
The moon forget her nightly tale,
And deepest silence hush on high
The radiant chorus of the sky.

4 But, fixed for everlasting years,
Unmoved amid the wrecks of spheres,
Thy word shall shine in cloudless day,
When heaven and earth have passed away.
                        Sir R. Grant.

BADEN. L. M.   THOS. HASTINGS.

1 I shall awake! however dread
    The shadows of the coming night;
Uprising from my dreamless bed,
    I shall again behold the light.

2 I shall awake! not of the earth,
    Whose ways with erring feet I've trod;
But fashioned by a glorious birth.
    Into the image of my God!

3 I shall awake! no more to crave
    With constant longing, still denied·
The good I covet I shall have;
    With Christ I shall be satisfied.

                  H. M. G. in "Zion's Herald."

WILLIAMS. L. M.   Arr. from Temple Carmina.

1 There is a land mine eye hath seen,
   In visions of enraptured thought,
  So bright that all that spreads between
   Is with its radiant glories fraught.

2 A land upon whose blissful shore,
   There rests no shadow, falls no stain;
  Where sin and sorrow vex no more,
   Eden is found on earth again.

3 Its skies are not like earthly skies,
   With varying hues of shade and light;
  It hath no need of suns to rise
   To dissipate the gloom of night.

4 There sweeps no desolating wind,
   Across that calm serene abode;
  All wanderers there a home may find,
   Within that paradise of God.
                    GURDON ROBINS.

GERMANY. L. M. BEETHOVEN.

1 He liveth long who liveth well,
   All other life is short and vain ;
  He liveth longest who can tell
   Of living most for heavenly gain.

2 He liveth long who liveth well.
   All else is life but flung away ;
  He liveth longest who can tell
   Of true things truly done each day.

3 Then fill the hours with what will last ;
   Buy up the moments as they go ;
  The life above, when this is past,
   Is the ripe fruit of life below.
                       H. BONAR.

ANGELS' CALL. S. M. — CHAS. BEECHER.

1 Blest are the pure in heart,
  For they shall see our God;
  The secret of the Lord is theirs;
  Their soul is Christ's abode.

2 Still to the lowly soul
  He doth Himself impart,
  And for His temple and His throne
  Chooseth the pure in heart.

3 Lord, we Thy presence seek,
  May ours this blessing be;
  O give the pure and lowly heart,
  A temple meet for Thee.

Rev. Jno. Keble, 1819.

PILGRIM. 8, 7.
Arr. from MOZART.

1 Tell me not in mournful numbers, Life is but an empty dream;
For the soul is dead that slumbers, And things are not what they seem.
Life is real, life is earnest, And the grave is not its goal:
Dust thou art, to dust returnest, Was not spoken of the soul.

2 Not enjoyment, and not sorrow,
　Is our destined end and way;
But to act that each to-morrow
　Finds us further than to-day.
Lives of true men all remind us,
　We can make our lives sublime;
And, departing, leave behind us
　Foot-prints on the sands of time.

3 Foot-prints, which, perhaps another,
　Sailing o'er life's solemn main.
A forlorn and shipwrecked brother,
　Seeing shall take heart again.
Let us, then, be up and doing,
　With a heart for any fate;
Still achieving, still pursuing.
　Learn to labor and to wait.
　　　　　　　　　LONGFELLOW.

ST. SACRAMENT, 10.

1 In the still air the music lies unheard!
  In the rough marble beauty hides unseen ;
To make the music and the beauty needs,
  The Master's touch, the sculptor's chisel keen,

2 Great Master, touch us with Thy skilful hand,
  Let not the music that is in us die ;
Great Sculptor, hew and polish us : nor let
  Hidden and Lost, Thy form within us lie !

3 Spare not the stroke ! do with us as Thou wilt.
  Let there be naught unfinished, broken, marred ;
Complete Thy purpose, that we may become
  Thy perfect image, Thou our God and Lord.

H. BONAR.

HOME, SWEET HOME. 11. Sir HENRY R. BISHOP.

1 'Mid pleas-ures and pal-a-ces, though we may roam,
Be it ev-er so hum-ble, there's no place [Omit] like home!
A charm from the skies seems to hal-low us here.
Which, seek thro' the world is ne'er met with elsewhere; Home, home,
sweet, sweet home, There's no place like home, There's no place like home.

2 An exile from home, splendor dazzles in vain!
Oh, give me my lowly thatched cottage again;
The birds singing gaily, that came at my call;
Oh, give me sweet peace of mind, dearer than all.
    Home, home, etc.

JOHN HOWARD PAYNE.

148 — WONDERFUL WORDS.

P. P. Bliss.

1 Sing them o-ver a-gain to me, Wonderful words of life;
Let me more of their beauty see, Wonderful words of life;
Words of life and beau-ty, Teach me faith and du-ty;

CHORUS.
Beau-ti-ful words, won-der-ful words, Won-der-ful words of life,
Beau-ti-ful words, won-der-ful words, Won-der-ful words of life.

2 Christ, the blessed One gives to all
  Wonderful words of life;
Sinner, list to the loving call,
  Wonderful words of life;
All so freely given,
Wooing us to heaven.—Cho.

3 Sweetly echo the gospel call,
  Wonderful words of life;
Offer pardon and peace to all,
  Wonderful words of life;
Jesus, only Savior,
Sanctify forever.—Cho.

P. P. Bliss.

1 This is the day of light :
Let there be light to-day ;
O Day-spring, rise upon our night,
And chase its gloom away.

2 This is the day of rest,
Our failing strength renew ;
On weary brain and troubled breast
Shed Thou Thy freshening dew.

3 This is the day of peace :
Thy peace our spirits fill
Bid Thou the blasts of discord cease
The waves of strife be still

4 This is the first of days :
Send forth Thy quickening Breath,
And wake dead souls to love and praise
O Vanquisher of death.
J. Ellerton.

GENERAL HYMNS.

COOLING. C. M.   ALONZO J. ABBEY. From TRIAD.

1 My heart is full of whispered song,
   My blindness is my sight;
The shadows that I feared so long
   Are all alive with light.

2 The while my pulses faintly beat,
   My faith doth so abound,
I feel grow firm beneath my feet,
   The green, immortal ground.

3 That Faith to me a courage gives
   Low as the grave to go ;
I know that my Redeemer lives,
   And that I live I know.

4 The palace walls I almost see.
   Where dwells my Lord and King ;
O grave, where is thy victory?
   O death, where is thy sting?
                      ALICE CARY, 1870.

GENERAL HYMNS.

CALEDONIA. 7, 7, 7, 6. Scotch

1 Soldiers of the cross, arise! Lo! your Leader from the skies Waves before you glory's prize, The prize of victory: Seize your armor, gird it on: Now the battle will be won; See, the strife will soon be done, Then struggle manfully.

2 Now the fight of faith begin,
Be no more the slaves of sin,
Strive the victor's palm to win,
　Trusting in the Lord:
Gird ye on the armor bright,
Warriors of the King of light,
Never yield, nor lose by flight
　Your divine reward.

3 Jesus conquered when He fell,
Met and vanquished death and
　hell;
Now He leads you on to swell
　The triumphs of His cross.

Though all earth and hell appear,
Who will doubt, or who can fear?
God, our strength and shield, is
　near;
We cannot lose our cause.

4 Onward, then, ye hosts of God!
Jesus points the victor's rod;
Follow where your Leader trod;
　You soon shall see His face.
Soon your enemies all slain,
Crowns of glory you shall gain,
Soon you'll join that glorious train
　Who shout their Savior's praise.

JARED B. WATERBURY.

152   GENERAL HYMNS.

NUREMBURG. 7.   Johann Rudolf Ahle, 1664.

1 Partners of a glorious hope!
   Lift your hearts and voices up;
   Nobly let us bear the strife,
   Keep the holiness, of Life.

2 Still forget the things behind,
   Follow God in heart and mind,
   To the mark unwearied press,
   Seize the crown of righteousness.

3 In our lives our faith be known,
   Faith by holy actions shown;
   Faith that mountains can remove,
   Faith that always works by love.
   Wesleyan.

ELMSWOOD. S. M. D.   Isaac B. Woodbury.

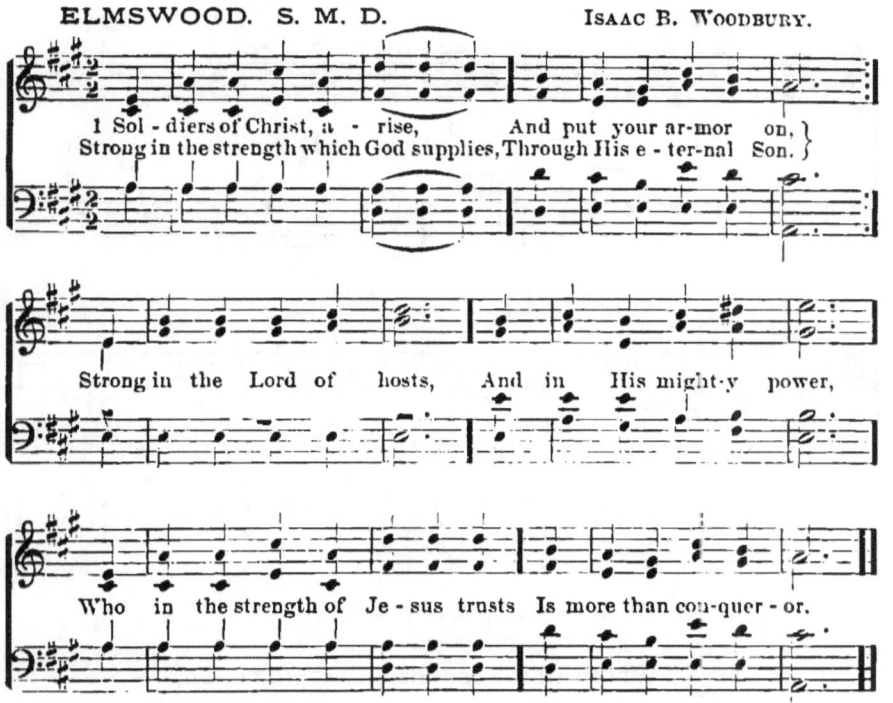

1 Soldiers of Christ, arise,
   And put your armor on,
Strong in the strength which God supplies,
   Through His eternal Son.
Strong in the Lord of hosts,
   And in His mighty power,
Who in the strength of Jesus trusts
   Is more than conqueror.

2 Stand, then, in His great might,
   With all His strength endued;
But take, to arm you for the fight,
   The panoply of God:
That, having all things done,
   And all your conflicts passed,
Ye may o'ercome through Christ alone,
   And stand entire at last.

3 Leave no unguarded place,
   No weakness of the soul;
Take every virtue, every grace,
   And fortify the whole:
Indissolubly joined,
   To battle all proceed;
But arm yourselves with all the mind
   That was in Christ, your Head.
                           Chas. Wesley.

BOYLSTON. S. M.   LOWELL MASON.

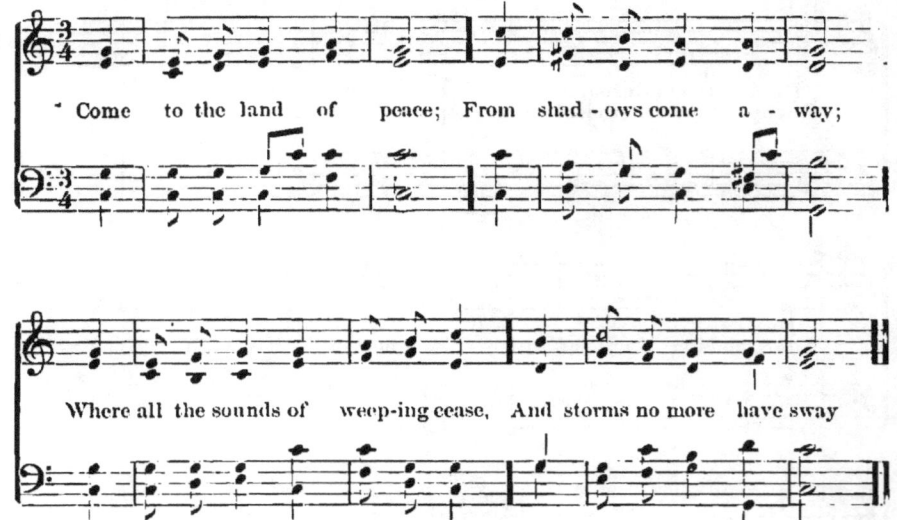

1 Come to the land of peace;
   From shadows come away;
 Where all the sounds of weeping cease,
   And storms no more have sway.

2 Fear hath no dwelling here;
   But pure repose and love
 Breathe through the bright, celestial air
   The spirit of the dove.

3 Come to the bright and blest,
   Gathered from every land;
 For here thy soul shall find its rest
   Amidst the shining band.

4 In this divine abode
   Change leaves no saddening trace;
 Come, trusting spirit, to thy God,
   Thy holy resting-place.

GENERAL HYMNS.

VIGIL. S. M.   St. Alban's Tune Book.

1 "Forever with the Lord!" Amen, so let it be!
Life from the dead is in that word, 'Tis immortality.

2 Here in the body pent,
  Absent from Thee I roam,
Yet nightly pitch my moving tent
  A day's march nearer home.

3 "Forever with the Lord!"
  Father, if 'tis Thy will,
The promise of Thy faithful word,
  E'en now and here fulfill.

4 So when my latest breath
  Shall rend the veil in twain,
By life I have escaped from death,
  And love eternal gain.

5 Knowing as I am known,
  How do I love that word,
And oft repeat before Thy throne,
  "Forever with the Lord!"

              J. Montgomery.

HENLEY. 11, 10.   LOWELL MASON.

1 Come unto Me, when shadows darkly gather,
  When the sad heart is weary and distressed,
Seeking for comfort from your heavenly Father,
  Come unto Me, and I will give you rest.

2 Large are the mansions in thy Father's dwelling,
  Glad are the homes that sorrows never dim;
Sweet are the harps in holy music swelling,
  Soft are the tones which raise the heavenly hymn.

3 There, like an Eden blossoming in gladness,
  Bloom the fair flowers the earth too rudely pressed;
Come unto Me, all ye who droop in sadness,
  Come unto Me, and I will give you rest.
              Mrs. Catherine H. Esling.

GENEVA. C. M.   J. COLE.

1 God's glory is a wondrous thing,
   Most strange in all its ways,
   And, of all things on earth, least like
   What men agree to praise.

2 Muse on His justice, downcast soul,
   Muse, and take better heart;
   Back with thine angel to the field,
   And bravely do thy part.

3 For Truth is Truth, and God is Good;
   And Truth the day must win;
   To doubt would be disloyalty,
   To falter would be sin!

FREDERICK W. FABER, 1849.

GENERAL HYMNS.

ST. AËLRED. 8, 8, 8, 3.

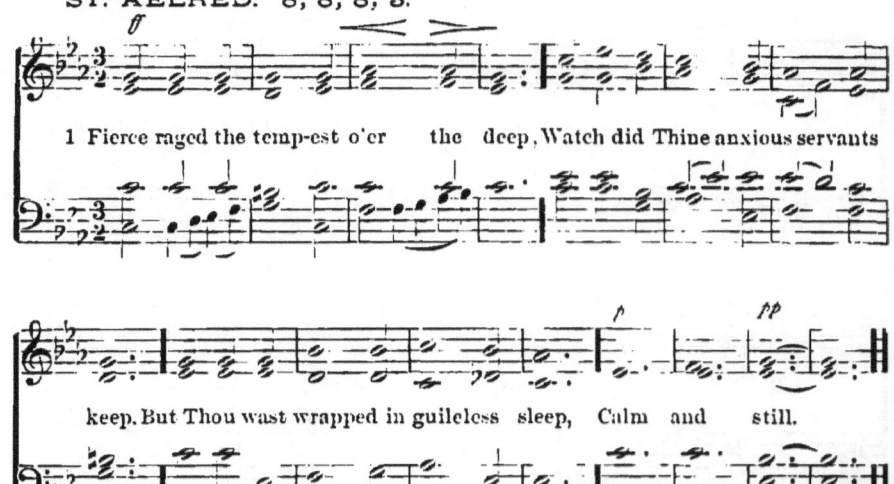

1 Fierce raged the tempest o'er the deep,
  Watch did Thine anxious servants keep,
  But Thou wast wrapped in guileless sleep,
    Calm and still.

2 "Save, Lord, we perish," was their cry,
  "O save us in our agony!"
  Thy word above the storm rose high,
    "Peace, be still."

3 The wild winds hushed; the angry deep
  Sank, like a little child, to sleep;
  The sullen billows ceased to leap,
    At Thy will.

4 So, when our life is clouded o'er,
  And storm-winds drift us from the shore,
  Say, lest we sink to rise no more,
    "Peace, be still."

ARCADIA. C. M.   T. HASTINGS.

1 We wait in faith, in prayer we wait, Until the happy hour, When God shall ope the morning gate, By His almighty power, By His almighty power.

2 We wait in faith, and turn our face
   To where the daylight springs,
Till He shall come, earth's gloom to chase,
   With healing on His wings.

3 And even now, amid the gray,
   The east is brightening fast,
And kindling to that perfect day,
   Which never shall be past.

4 We wait in faith, we wait in prayer,
   Till that blest day shall shine,
When earth shall fruits of Eden bear,
   And all, O God, be Thine.

5 O guide us till our night is done!
   Until, from shore to shore,
Thou Lord, our everlasting sun.
   Art shining evermore.

                    SAMUEL LONGFELLOW, 1848.

MISSIONARY CHANT. L. M.   H. C. ZEUNER.

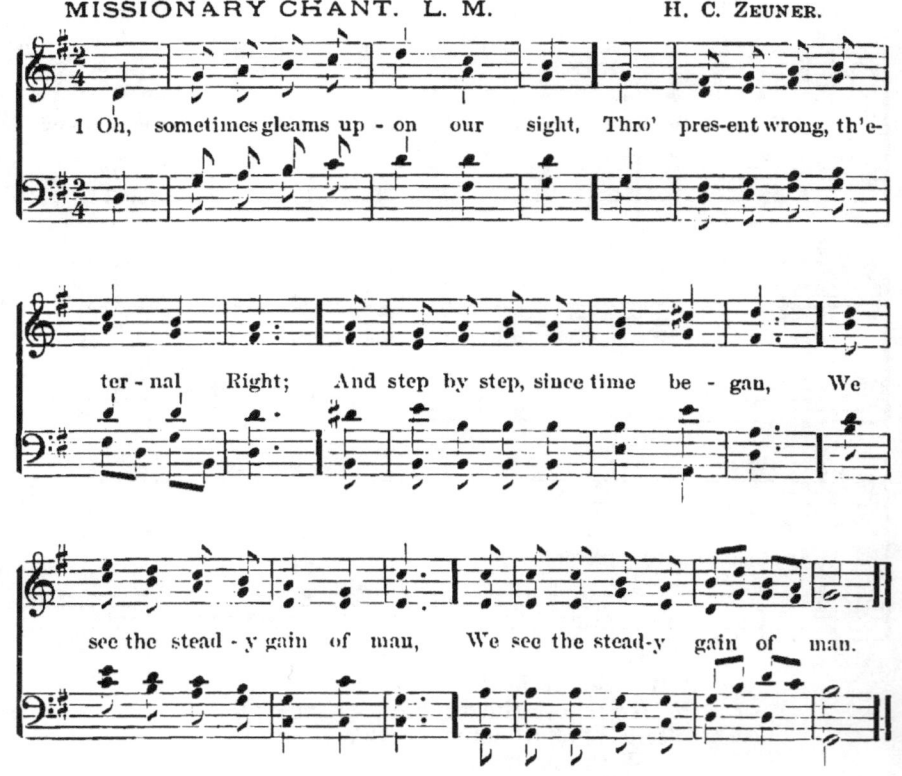

1 Oh, sometimes gleams upon our sight, Thro' present wrong, th' eternal Right; And step by step, since time began, We see the steady gain of man, We see the steady gain of man.

2 That all of good the past hath had
Remains to make our own time glad,
Our common, daily life divine,
And every land a Palestine.

3 Through the harsh noises of our day.
A low, sweet prelude finds its way;
Thro' clouds of doubt, and creeds of fear,
A light is breaking calm and clear.

4 Henceforth my heart shall sigh no more
For olden time and holier shore:
God's love and blessing, then and there
Are now, and here, and everywhere.
                   J. G. WHITTIER.

JANES. L. M.   J. C. W. A. Mozart.

1. Abide not in the realm of dreams,
O man, however fair it seems;
But with clear eye the present scan,
And hear the call of God and man.

2. Think not in sleep to fold thy hands,
Forgetful of thy Lord's commands;
From duty's claims no life is free,
Behold, to-day hath need of Thee!

3. While the day lingers, do thy best;
Full soon the night will bring its rest
And, duty done, that rest shall be
Full of beatitudes to thee.

                           Wm. H. Burleigh.

NAUFORD. 8, 8, 8, 4.   Sir. ARTHUR S. SULLIVAN.

1 Oh, backward looking son of time.
    The new is old, the old is new;
  The cycle of a change sublime
    Still sweeping through.

2 Take heart! the Master builds again,
    A charmed life old Goodness hath;
  The tares may perish, but the grain
    Is not for death.

3 God works in all things, all obey
    His first propulsion from the night;
  Ho, wake and watch! the world is gray
    With morning light!

                    J. G. WHITTIER.

HERSAL. C. M.   W. LOCKETT.

1 The harp at Na-ture's ad-vent strung Has nev-er ceased to play;

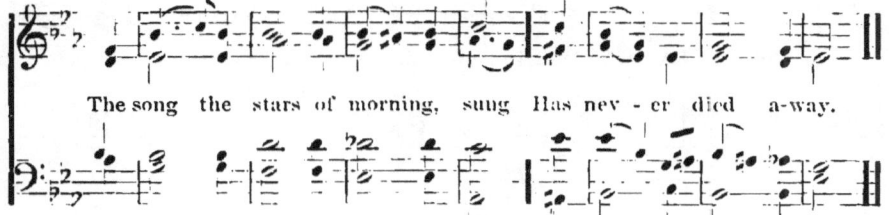

The song the stars of morning, sung Has nev-er died a-way.

1 The harp at Nature's advent strung
   Has never ceased to play :
The song the stars of morning sung
   Has never died away,

2 And prayer is made, and praise is given
   By all things near and far :
The ocean looketh up to heaven,
   And mirrors every star.

3 The green earth sends her incense up
   From many a mountain shrine ·
From folded leaf and dewy cup
   She pours her sacred wine.

4 So Nature keeps the reverent frame,
   With which her years began ;
And all her signs and voices shame
   A prayerless heart in man.
                     J. G. WHITTIER.

ST. PETERSBURG. L. M. — BORTNIANSKY.

1 When gath'ring clouds around I view,
And days are dark, and friends are few,
On Him I lean, who not in vain
Experienced every human pain;
He sees my wants, allays my fears,
And counts and treasures up my tears

2 If aught should tempt my sense to stray
From heavenly wisdom's narrow way,
To fly the good I would pursue,
Or do the wrong I would not do,
Still He who felt temptation's power
Will guard me in that dangerous hour.
                                    ROBERT GRANT.

BLUMENTHAL. 7, D.   JACOB BLUMENTHAL.

1 Children of the heav'n-ly King,
As we journey let us sing:
Sing our Savior's worthy praise,
Glorious in His works and ways:
O ye banished seed, be glad;
Christ our Advocate is made:
Us to save our flesh assumes,
Brother to our souls becomes.

2 Fear not, brethren, joyful stand
On the borders of our land;
Jesus Christ, our Father's Son,
Bids us undismayed go on;
Lord, obediently we'll go,
Gladly leaving all below:
Only Thou our Leader be,
And we still will follow Thee.
                    JOHN CENNICK.

GOD IS LOVE. 7.

English.

1 See the ransomed million stand, Palms of conquest in their hands!
This before the throne their strain, "Hell is vanquished, death is slain!"

1 See the ransomed millions stand,
  Palms of conquest in their hands!
  This before the throne their strain,
  "Hell is vanquished, death is slain!"

2 "Blessing, honor, glory, might,
  Are the Conqueror's native right!
  Thrones and powers before Him fall
  Lamb of God, and Lord of all!"

3 Hasten, Lord! the promised hour;
  Come in glory and in power!
  Still Thy foes are unsubdued:
  Nature sighs to be renewed.

4 Time has nearly reached its sum:
  All things with the Bride, say, "Come!"
  Jesus! whom all worlds adore,
  Come, and reign forevermore!

CONDER.

AMERICA. 6, 4.   HENRY CAREY.

1 My country! 'tis of thee, Sweet land of liberty, Of thee I sing: Land where my fathers died! Land of the pilgrims' pride! From ev'ry mountain side Let freedom ring!

2 Let music swell the breeze,
And ring from all the trees
Sweet freedom's song:
Let mortal tongues awake;
Let all that breathe partake;
Let rocks their silence break,
The sound prolong.

3 Our fathers' God! to Thee,
Author of liberty,
To Thee we sing:
Long may our land be bright
With freedom's holy light;
Protect us by Thy might,
Great God, our King!

S. F. SMITH.

VIGILATE. 7, 7, 7, 3.

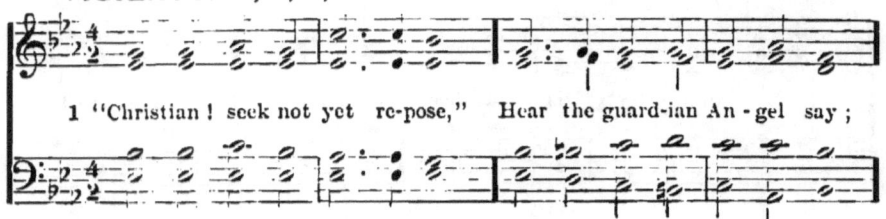

1 "Christian! seek not yet re-pose," Hear the guard-ian An-gel say;

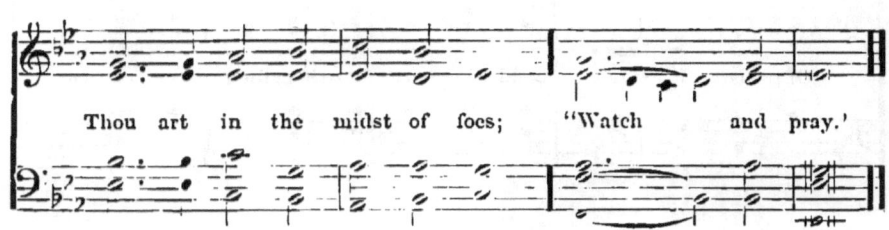

Thou art in the midst of foes; "Watch and pray."

2 Principalities and powers,
   Mustering their unseen array,
Wait for thy unguarded hours:
   "Watch and pray."

3 Gird thy heavenly armor on,
   Wear it ever night and day;
Ambushed lies the evil one;
   "Watch and pray."

4 Hear the victors who o'ercame;
   Still they mark each warrior's way;
All with one sweet voice exclaim,
   "Watch and pray."

5 Hear, above all, hear thy Lord,
   Him thou lovest to obey;
Hide within thy heart His Word,
   "Watch and pray."

GENERAL HYMNS.

BENJAMIN. S. M.   FRANCIS J. HAYDN.

1 Pray, without ceasing pray, Your Captain gives the word; His summons cheerfully obey, And call upon the Lord, And call upon the Lord.

2 To God your every want
   In instant prayer display;
Pray always; pray, and never faint;
   Pray, without ceasing pray.

3 In fellowship, alone,
   To God with faith draw near;
Approach His courts, besiege His throne,
   And know the power of prayer.

4 From strength to strength go on;
   Wrestle, and fight and pray;
Tread all the powers of darkness down,
   You'll win the well-fought day.

5 Still let the Spirit cry
   Through all His soldiers, "Come!"
Till Christ the Lord descend from high,
   And take the conquerors home.
                  CHARLES WESLEY.

RETREAT. L. M.   THOS. HASTINGS.

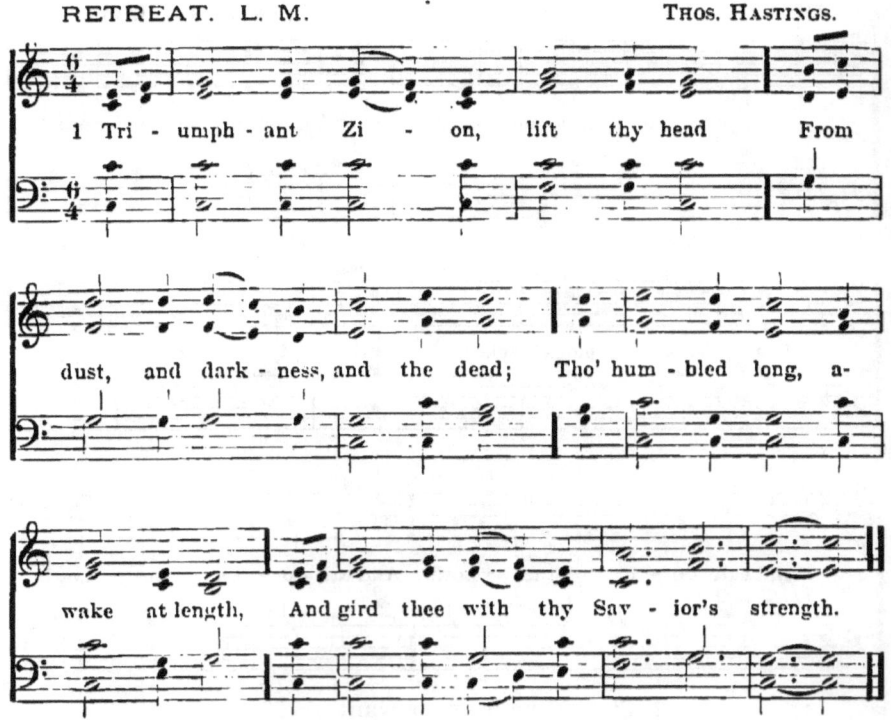

1 Triumphant Zion, lift thy head
From dust, and darkness, and the dead;
Tho' humbled long, awake at length,
And gird thee with thy Savior's strength.

2 Put all thy beauteous garments on,
And let thy excellence be known:
Decked in the robes of righteousness,
The world thy glories shall confess.

3 No more shall foes unclean invade,
And fill thy hallowed walls with dread;
No more shall hell's insulting host
Their victory and thy sorrows boast.

4 God, from on high, has heard thy prayer;
His hand thy ruins shall repair;
Nor will thy watchful monarch cease
To guard thee in eternal peace.
                           DODDRIDGE.

MILWAUKEE. 8, 7.   John Zundel.

1 Holy Spirit, Source of gladness,
Come with all thy radiance bright;
O'er our weariness and sadness,
Breathe Thy life and shed Thy light.

2 Send us thine illumination,
   Banish all our fears at length ;
Rest upon this congregation,
   Spirit of unfailing strength.

3 Let that love which knows no measure,
   Now in quickening showers descend,
Bringing us the richest treasure
   Man can wish or God can send.

4 Hear our earnest supplication ;
   Every struggling heart release ;
Rest upon this congregation,
   Spirit of untroubled Peace.
                              Anon.

CHRYSOLITE. L. M.
S. B. Pond.

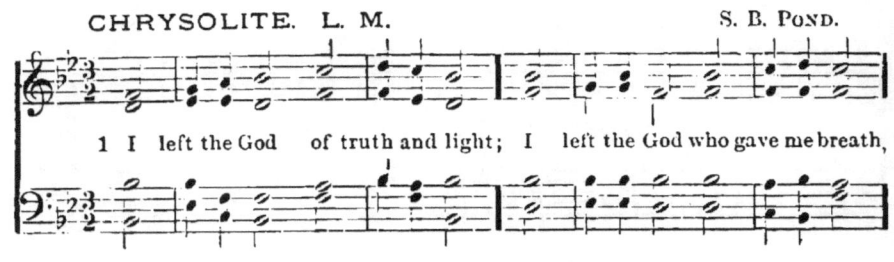

1 I left the God of truth and light; I left the God who gave me breath,

To wan-der in the wilds of night, And per-ish in the snares of death

2 In riches when I sought for joy,
   And placed in sordid gains my trust,
I found that gold was all alloy,
   And worldly treasures fleeting dust.

3 I wooed ambition, climbed the pole,
   And shone among the stars, but fell
Headlong in all my pride of soul,
   Like Lucifer, from heaven to hell.

4 Lo, through the gloom of guilty fears.
   My faith discerns a dawn of grace;
The Sun of Righteousness appears
   In Jesus' reconciling face.

5 My suffering, slain and risen Lord,
   In sore distress I turn to Thee;
I claim acceptance on Thy word,
   My God! my God! Thou lovest me.

                   Montgomery.

WOODLAND. C. M.   N. D. GOULD.

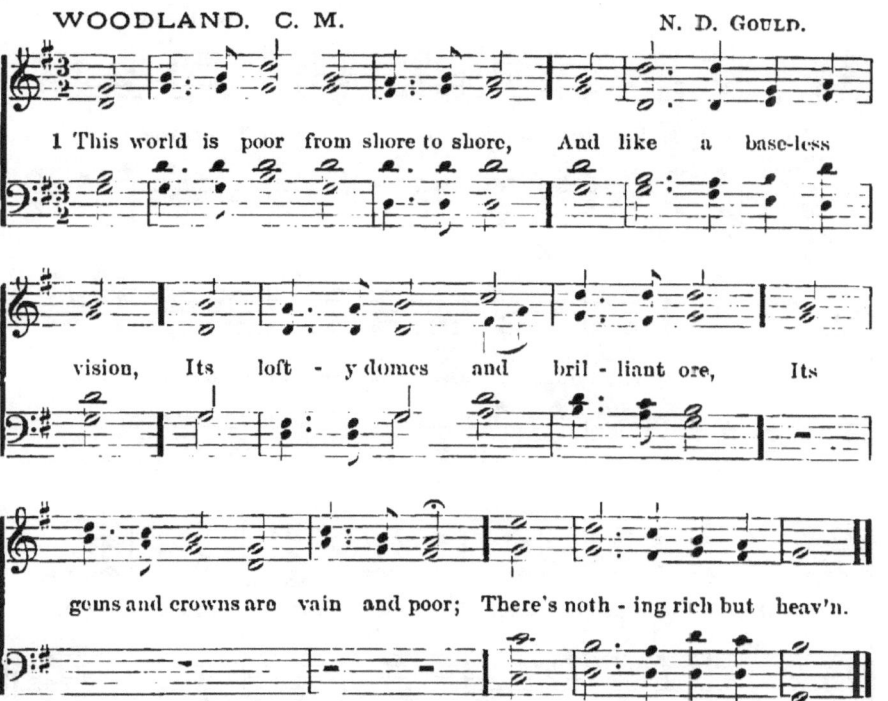

1 This world is poor from shore to shore, And like a base-less vision, Its loft-y domes and bril-liant ore, Its gems and crowns are vain and poor; There's noth-ing rich but heav'n.

2 Empire decay, and nations die,
   Our hopes to winds are given;
The vernal blooms in ruin lie,
Death reigns o'er all beneath the sky;
   There's nothing sure but heaven.

3 Creations mighty fabric all
   Shall be to atoms riven;
The skies consume, the planets fall,
Convulsions rock the earthly ball,
   There's nothing firm but heaven.

4 The clouds disperse, the light appears,
   My sins are all forgiven;
Triumphant grace has quelled my fears;
Roll on thou sun, fly swift, my years,
   I'm on my way to heaven.
                     Unknown.

GENERAL HYMNS.

FOSTER. 8.   W. B. BRADBURY.

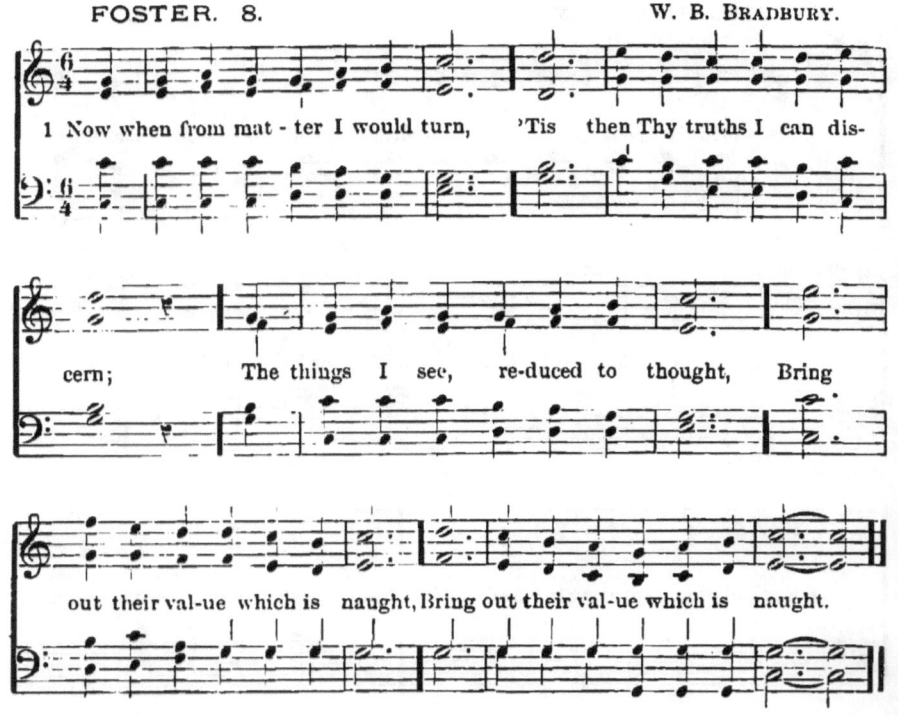

1 Now when from matter I would turn,
  'Tis then Thy truths I can discern;
  The things I see, reduced to thought,
  Bring out their value, which is naught.

2 Then glance whichever way I will,
  I see Thy glories round me still;
  I see them shining out so clear,
  That love now takes the place of fear.

3 And now I see the prize is mine,
  And know the crown will ever shine;
  I know the Truth comes from above,
  From Him, the Life, and Truth and Love.
                       F. E. MASON.

ALABASTER. S. M.   PLEYEL.

2 My longing eyes look out,
    For Thy enlivening ray ;
  More duly than the morning watch,
    To spy the dawning day.

3 Let Isarel trust in God,
    No bounds His mercy knows;
  The plenteous source and spring from whence
    Eternal succor flows.

4 Whose friendly streams to us
    Supplies, in want convey ;
  A healing spring, a spring to cleanse,
    And wash our guilt away.

HE LEADETH ME. L. M. — WM. B. BRADBURY.

1 He lead-eth me! O blessed thought! O words with heav'nly comfort fraught;
Whate'er I do, where'er I be, Still 'tis God's hand that leadeth me.

CHORUS.
He lead-eth me, He lead-eth me, By His own hand He lead-eth me:
His faith-ful fol-low-er I would be, For by His hand He lead-eth me.

2 Lord, I would clasp Thy hand in mine,
  Nor ever murmur nor repine;
  Content, whatever lot I see,
  Since 'tis my God that leadeth me!—Cho.

3 And when my task on earth is done,
  When, by Thy grace, the victory's won,
  E'en death's cold wave, I will not flee,
  Since God through Jordan leadeth me.—Cho.

J. H. GILMORE.

GENERAL HYMNS. 177

CHRISTUS CONSOLATOR. 8, 5, 8, 3

1 Art thou weary, art thou languid, Art thou sore distrest?
"Come to Me," saith One, "and coming Be at rest!"

2 Hath He marks to lead me to Him,
  If He be my guide?
"In His feet and hands are wound-prints,
  And His side."

3 Hath He diadem as Monarch
  That His brow adorns?
"Yes, a crown, in very surety,
  But of thorns."

4 If I find Him, if I follow,
  What His guerdon here?
"Many a sorrow, many a labor,
  Many a tear."

5 If I still hold closely to Him,
  What hath He at last?
"Sorrow vanquished, labor ended,
  Jordan past."

6 If I ask Him to receive me,
  Will He say me nay?
"Not till earth, and not till heaven
  Pass away."

7 Finding, following, keeping, struggling,
  Is He sure to bless?
"Angels, Martyrs, Prophets, Virgins,
  Answer, Yes!"

178   GENERAL HYMNS.

TANTUM ERGO. 8, 7, 4.   From the "Memorare." Dr. WILCOX.

1 We the weak ones, we the sinners,
Would not in our poorness stay;
We the low ones would be winners
Of what holy height we may;
Ever nearer, ever nearer,
To Thy pure and perfect day.

2 Shall things withered, fashions olden,
Keep us from life's flowing spring?
Waits for us the promise golden,
Waits each new diviner thing;
Onward, onward,
Why this faithless tarrying.

3 By each saving word unspoken;
By Thy truth, as yet half won;
By each idol yet unbroken;
By Thy will, yet poorly done;
Hear us, hear us,
Thou Almighty! help us on.

4 Nearer to Thee would we venture,
Of Thy truth more largely take,
Upon life diviner enter,
Into day more glorious break,
To the ages, to the ages,
Fair bequests and costly make.

THOMAS H. GILL, 1869.

HURSLEY. L. M. HAYDN, 1798.
Arr. by Wm. H. Monk, 1861.

1 "Let there be light," thus spake the Word. The Word was God, "and there was light;"

Still that cre-a-tive voice is heard, And day a-ris-es from each night.

1 "Let there be light," thus spake the Word.
  The Word was God "and there was light;"
  Still that creative voice is heard,
  And day arises from each night.

2 And every night shall turn to day,
  While months, and years and ages roll;
  And science turns a brighter ray
  Down in the chaos of the soul.

3 Nor this alone, its wakening smiles
  Break on the gloom of pagan sleep;
  The Word hath reached the utmost isles,
  God's Spirit moves upon the deep.

4 Already from the dust of death,
  Man in his Makers's image, stands;
  Always inhales immortal breath,
  And stretches forth to heaven his hands.

MONTGOMERY.

SOMERVILLE. L. M.

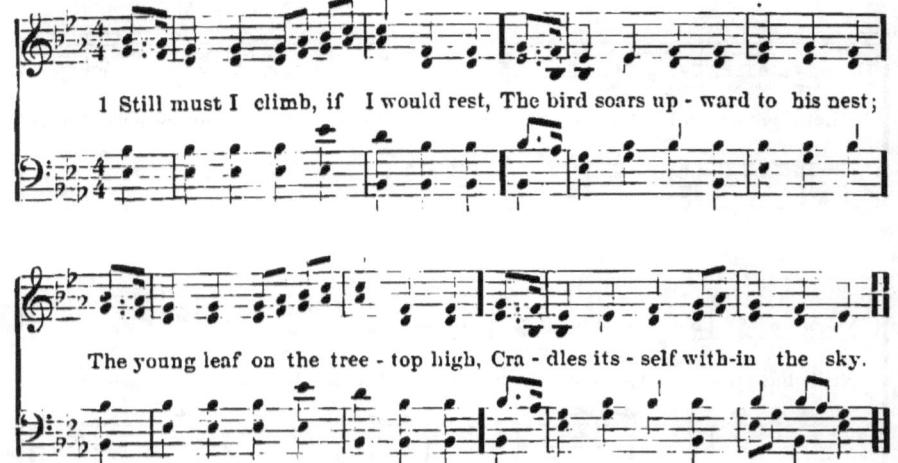

1 Still must I climb, if I would rest,
The bird soars upward to his nest;
The young leaf on the tree-top high,
Cradles itself within the sky.

2 The streams that seem to hasten down,
Return in clouds the hills to crown;
The plant arises from her root,
To rock aloft her flower and fruit.

3 I cannot in the valley stay;
The great horizons stretch away,
The very cliffs that wall me round
Are ladders unto higher ground.

4 To work, to rest for each a time,
I toil, but I must also climb;
What soul was ever quite at ease,
Shut in by earthly boundaries.

5 I am not glad till I have known,
Life that can lift me from my own;
A loftier level must be won,
A mightier strength to lean upon.

6 And heaven draws near as I ascend,
The breeze invites, the stars befriend,
All things are beckoning to the best,
I climb to Thee, my God, for rest.

LUCY LARCOM.

PETERBOROUGH. C. M. R. HARRISON, 1786.

1 Oh, still in accents sweet and strong
   Sounds forth the ancient word,
   "More reapers for white harvest fields,
   More laborers for the Lord!"

2 We hear the call; in dreams no more
   In selfish ease we lie,
   But girded for our Father's work,
   Go forth beneath His sky.

3 Where prophets' word, and martyrs' blood,
   And prayers of saints are sown,
   We, to their labors entering in,
   Would reap where they have strown.
   SAMUEL LONGFELLOW.

GENERAL HYMNS.

VOX DILECTI. C. M. D.

1 I heard the voice of Jesus say, "Come unto Me and rest;
Lay down, thou weary one, lay down Thy head upon My Breast:"
I came to Jesus as I was, Weary, and worn, and sad;
I found in Him a resting-place, And He has made me glad.

2 I heard the voice of Jesus say,
   "Behold, I freely give
The living water, thirsty one.
   Stoop down, and drink, and
I came to Jesus, and I drank [live;"
   Of that life-giving stream;
My thirst was quenched, my soul
   revived.
And now I live in Him.

3 I heard the voice of Jesus say,
   "I am this dark world's Light:
Look unto Me, thy morn shall rise,
   And all thy day be bright:"
I looked to Jesus, and I found
   In Him my Star, my Sun;
And in that Light of life I'll walk
   Till travelling days are done.

H. BONAR.

GENERAL HYMNS. 183

JEWETT. 6.   Arr. from C. M. WEBER, by J. P. HOLBROOK.

1 Ye know God but as Lord, Hence, Lord, His name with thee Oh, know Him but as Love And, Love His name will be; He rose not from the dead, He still is in the grave, If thou, for whom He died, Art still of sin the slave.

2 In all Eternity,
   No love can be so sweet
As when man's heart with God
   In unison doth beat;
Whate'er thou lovest, man,
   That, too, become thou must;
God, if thou lovest God,
   Dust, if thou lovest dust.

3 The cross on Golgotha
   Can never serve thy soul,
The cross in thine own heart
   Alone can make thee whole,
Infinite Creator
   Who on earth, but knows it,
And yet a human heart
   Can perfectly enclose it.
          ANGELUS SILISCUS, 1620.

CLINTON. C. M.   J. P. HOLBROOK.

1 When I can read my title clear
  To mansions in the skies,
I bid farewell to every fear,
  And wipe my weeping eyes.

2 Should earth against my soul engage,
  And firey darts be hurled,
Then I can smile at Satan's rage,
  And face a frowning world.

3 Let cares like a wild deluge come,
  And storms of sorrow fall,
So I but safely reach my home,
  My God, my heaven, my all.

4 There I shall bathe my weary soul
  In seas of heavenly rest,
And not a wave of trouble roll
  Across my peaceful breast
                ISAAC WATTS.

DULCETTA. 8, 7.   From LUDWIG VON BEETHOVEN.

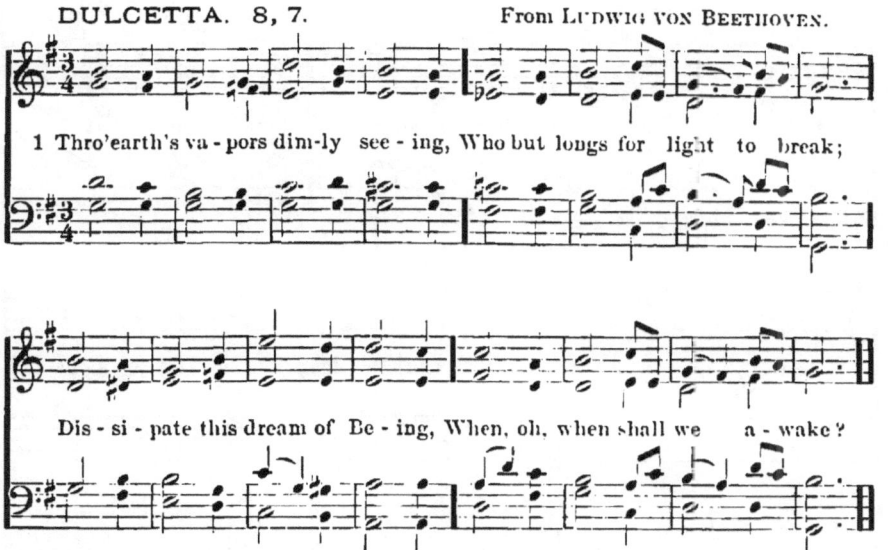

1. Through earth's vapors dimly seeing,
   Who but longs for light to break;
   Dissipate this dream of Being,
   When, oh, when shall we awake

2. Oh, the time when this material
   Shall have vanished like a cloud,
   And amid the wide ethereal,
   All the Spiritual shall crowd.

3. Naked stand, but still surrounded
   With realities unknown;
   Triumph in the view unbounded,
   Know ourselves "as we are known."

4. In that sudden strange transition,
   By what new and glorious sense,
   Shall we grasp the mighty vision,
   And receive its influence.

ST. THOMAS. S. M. — GEORGE F. HANDEL.

1 Green pastures and clear streams,
Freedom and quiet rest,
Christ's flock enjoy, beneath His beams,
Or in His shadow, blest.

2 The mountain and the vale,
Forest and field, they range;
The morning dew, the evening gale,
Bring health in every change.

3 Should storms of trouble blow,
Warned of the coming shock,
They to the Rock of Ages go;
Their Shepherd is their Rock.

4 Conflicts and trials done,
His glory they behold,
Where Jesus and His flock are one,
One Sheperd and one fold.

MONTGOMERY.

ELLACOMBE. 7, 6.   ST. GALL.

1 Now is the time approach-ing, By prophets long foretold, When all shall dwell together; One Shepherd and one fold, Now Jew and Gentile, meeting From many a distant shore, Around one altar kneeling, One common Lord adore.

    2 Let all that now divides us,
       Remove and pass away,
    Like shadows of the midnight
       Before the blaze of day;
    And all that now unites us
       More sweet and lasting prove,
    A closer bond of union,
       A closer bond of love.

    3 O long-expected dawning,
       O bright and cheering ray.
    Before thy warmth and brightness,
       The shadows flee away;
    This glad anticipation.
       It cheers the toilers on
    To watch, and hope, and labor,
       Till the dark night be gone.
                  JANE BORTHWICK. 1863.

CHESHIRE. C. M.

1 Beneath the shadow of the cross,
  As earthly hopes remove,
His new commandment Jesus gives,
  His blessed word of love.

2 A bond of union strong and deep,
  A bond of perfect peace;
Not even the lifted cross can harm,
  If we but hold to this.

3 Then, Jesus, be thy Spirit ours;
  And swift our feet shall move,
To deeds of pure self sacrifice.
  And the sweet tasks of love.
                    SAMUEL LONGFELLOW.

AUSTRIA. 8, 7, D. FRANCIS J. HAYDN.

1 Glorious things of thee are spoken, Zion, city of our God;
He, whose word cannot be broken, Formed thee for His own abode;
On the Rock of ages founded, What can shake thy sure repose?
With salvation's walls surrounded, Thou mayst smile at all thy foes.

2 See, the streams of living waters,
   Springing from eternal love,
Still supply Thy sons and daughters,
   And all fear of want remove:
Who can faint while such a river
   Ever flows our thirst to assuage?
Grace. which, like the Lord, the giver,
   Never fails from age to age.

3 Round each habitation hovering,
   See the cloud and fire appear,
For a glory and a covering,
   Showing that the Lord is near!
He who gives us daily manna,
   He who listens when we cry,
Let him hear the loud hossana
   Rising to His throne on high.
               JOHN NEWTON.

THE LORD WILL PROVIDE. H. M.

C. S. Harrington, by per. E. Tourjee.

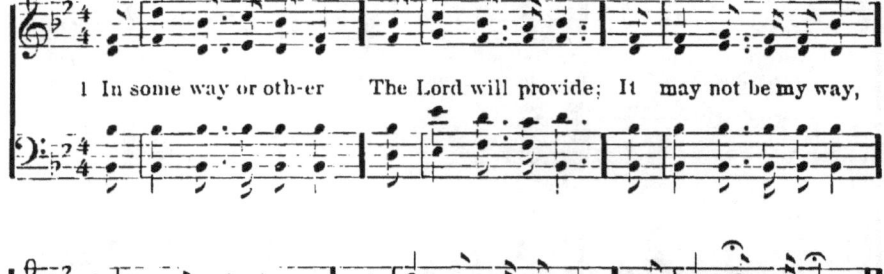

1 In some way or other
The Lord will provide;
It may not be my way,
It may not be thy way,
And yet, in His own way
"The Lord will provide."

2 At some time or other
The Lord will provide
It may not be my time,
It may not be thy time,
And yet, in His own time,
"The Lord will provide."

3 Despond, then, no longer:
The Lord will provide;
And this be the token,
No word He hath spoken
Was ever yet broken,
"The Lord will provide."

4 March on, then, right boldly;
The sea shall divide;
The pathway made glorious,
With shoutings victorious,
We'll join in the chorus,
"The Lord will provide."

Mrs. M. A. W. Cooke.

HENDON. 7. H. A. C. MALAN, 1830.

1 Slowly o'er the sleeping world.
  Nature's curtains are unfurled;
  Veiling days, distracting sights,
  Showing heaven's eternal lights.

2 Living stars to view are brought,
  In the boundless realms of thought;
  High and infinite desires,
  Flaming like those upper fires,

3 Holy Truth, Eternal Right,
  Let them break upon our sight;
  Let them shine serene and still,
  And with light my being fill.

W. H. FURNESS, 1840.

COME, YE DISCONSOLATE. 11. 10.

WEBBE, of England.

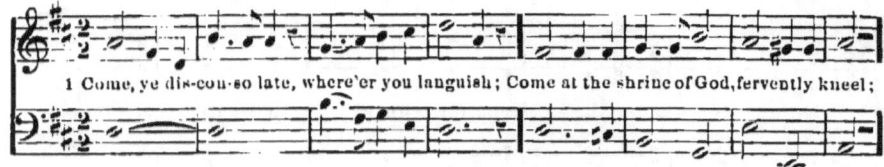
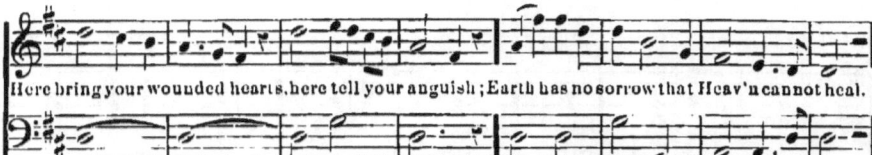

1 Come, ye disconsolate, where'er you languish,
   Come at the shrine of God, fervently kneel;
  Here bring your wounded hearts, here tell your anguish,
   Earth has no sorrow that Heaven cannot heal.

2 Joy of the desolate, light of the straying,
   Hope of the penitent, fadeless and pure,
  Here speaks the Comforter, tenderly saying,
   "Earth has no sorrow that Heaven cannot cure."

3 Here see the bread of life ; see waters flowing
   Forth from the throne of God, pure from above;
  Come to the feast of love ; come ever knowing
   Earth has no sorrow but Heaven can remove.

THOMAS MOORE.

RUSSIAN HYMN. 10.   Russian National Air.

1 Rise crown'd with light, im-pe-rial Sa-lem, rise, Ex-alt thy tower-ing head, and lift thine eyes; See heav'n, its sparkling port-als wide dis-play, And break up-on thee in a flood of day.

2 See a long race, thy spacious courts adorn,
See future sons and daughters yet unborn,
In crowding ranks on every side arise,
Demanding life, impatient for the skies.

3 See barbarous nations at thy gates attend,
Walk in thy light, and in thy temple bend,
See thy bright altars throng'd with prostrate Kings,
While every land its joyous tribute brings.

4 The sea shall waste, the skies to smoke decay,
Rocks fall to dust and mountains melt away;
But fixed His word, His saving power remains;
Thy realm shall last, Thy own Messiah reigns.

ALEXAND: R POPE.

REDEMPTOR MUNDI. 10.

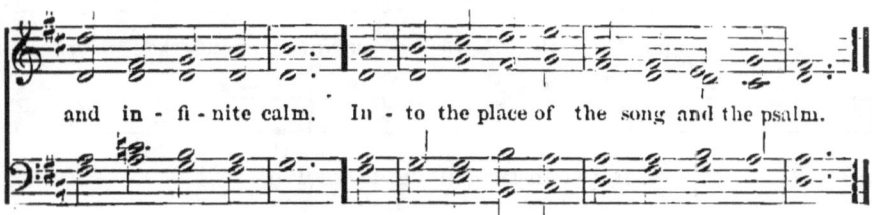

1 Out of the distance, and darkness so deep,
Out of the settled and perilous sleep,
Into the quiet and infinite calm,
Into the place of the song and the psalm.

2 Out of disaster and ruin complete,
Out of the struggle and dreary defeat,
Into a righteous and permanent peace,
Into to the grandest and fullest release.

3 Out of the bondage and wearying chains,
Out of companionship ever with pains.
Into communion with Father and Son,
Into the sharing of all that Christ won.

4 Wonderful love, that has wrought all for me;
Wonderful work that has thus set me free;
Wonderful ground upon which I have come;
Wonderful tenderness welcoming home.

GENERAL HYMNS.

OLIVET. 6, 4.   LOWELL MASON.

1 Between two seas we stand, One is on either hand; Matter and soul One is the sea of naught, The other's life is caught, The other's life is caught, From mind, the whole.

2 Between two thoughts we live,
  One from our Lord, doth give
    Freedom sublime;
  The other from His foe,
||: Comes with all mortal woe, :||
    And stings of time.

3 Between two worlds we move,
  One from the real doth prove;
    One from the dust;
  In spirit, if we bide,
||: Not to the unreal tied. :||
    We safely trust.

4 Between the earth and sky,
  A million insects ply,
    Their daily task;
  So men may toil in sin,
||: Or they may soar, and, in :||
    God's sunlight bask.

KELLEY. 8, 7.

1 Peace be to this congregation!
  Peace to every heart therein!
Peace the earnest of salvation,
  Peace the fruit of conquered sin!
Peace that speaks the heavenly Giver!
  Peace the worldly minds unknown,
Peace that floweth like a river,
  From the eternal Source alone.

2 O thou God of Peace, be near us,
  Fix within our hearts, Thy home;
With Thy bright-appearing cheer us,
  In Thy blessed freedom come;
Come with all Thy revelations,
  Truth which we so long have sought;
Come with Thy deep consolations,
  Peace of God which passeth thought.
                                Wesleyan.

198   TRUTH.

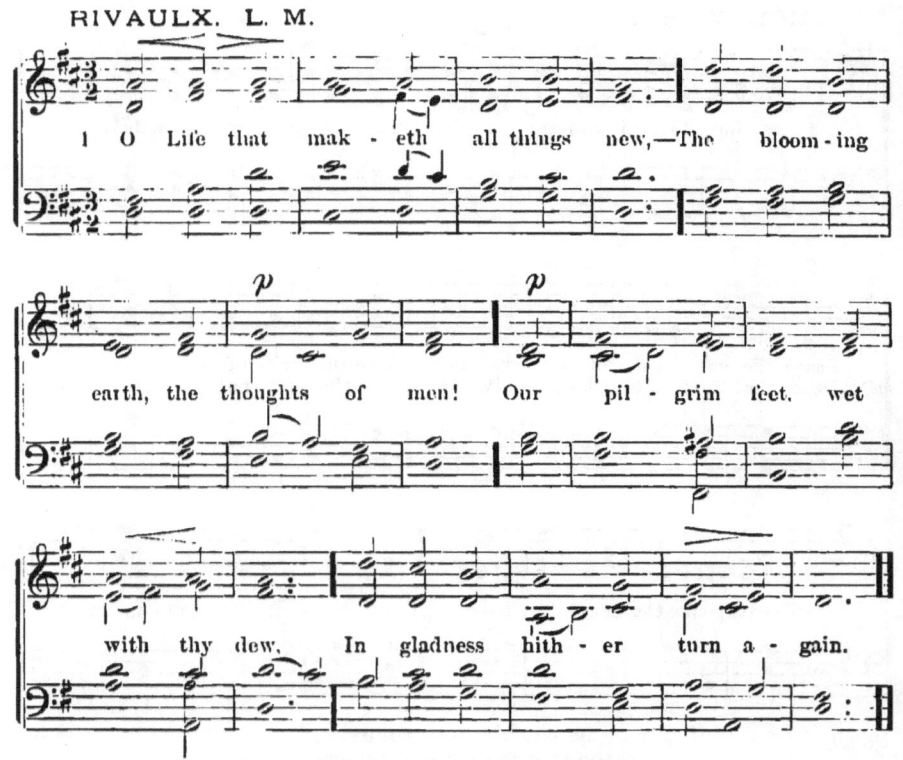

RIVAULX. L. M.

1 O Life that mak-eth all things new,—The blooming earth, the thoughts of men! Our pilgrim feet, wet with thy dew, In gladness hither turn again.

2 From hand to hand the greeting flows,
  From eye to eye the signals run,
  From heart to heart the bright hope glows;
  The seekers of the Light are one.

3 One in the freedom of the truth,
  One in the joy of paths untrod,
  One in the soul's perennial youth,
  One in the larger thought of God

4 The freer step, the fuller breath,
  The wide horizon's grander view,
  The sense of life that knows no death,—
  The Life that maketh all things new.

                            SAMUEL LONGFELLOW.

TRUTH. 199

BADEA. S. M.   German Melody.

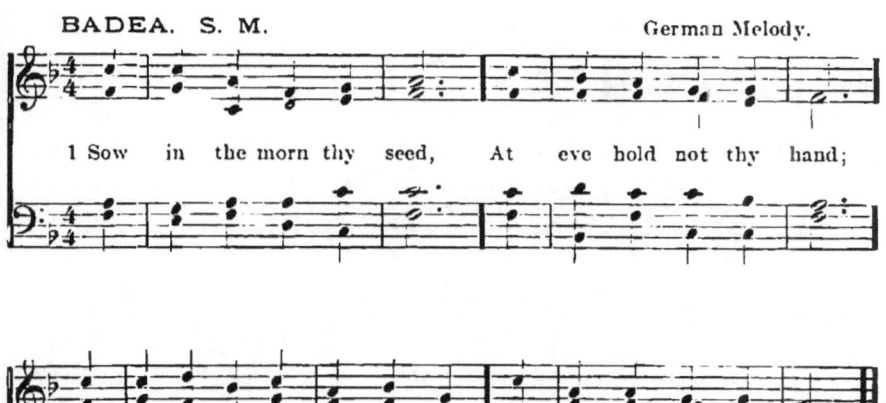

1 Sow in the morn thy seed, At eve hold not thy hand; To doubt and fear give thou no heed, Broad-cast it o'er the land.

1 Sow in the morn thy seed,
    At eve hold not thy hand;
  To doubt and fear give thou no heed,
    Broad-cast it o'er the land.

2 Beside all waters sow,
    The highway furrows stock,
  Drop it where thorns and thistles grow,
    Scatter it on the rock.

3 And duly shall appear,
    In verdure, beauty, strength,
  The tender blade, the stalk, the ear;
    And the full corn at length.

TRUTH.

ORIENT. 11, 10.   MOZART.

1. I thank Thee, O God; for the glorious light,
   The light that is Truth, and dispels the night;
   I thank Thee for Jesus, His words I would cite,
   "Your nets you must cast on the side of the right."

2. I thank Thee for her who divided the sea,
   Showed me the way out of bondage to flee;
   This way she is leading, tho' narrow must be
   The way I must follow to come to Thee.

3. I thank Thee for wisdom that cometh from Thee,
   Footprints of Jesus, the way I can see;
   I thank Thee, O Life, Love, and Truth, for these Three.
   Teach of heaven, the Glory that's waiting for me.

FRANK E. MASON, C. S. B.

TRUTH.

PORTUGUESE HYMN. 11. MARCIS PORTIGOLLO.

1 How firm a foun-da-tion, ye saints of the Lord, Is laid for your faith in His excellent word! What more can He say, than to you He hath said, To you, who for ref-uge to Je-sus have fled? To you, who for ref-uge to Je-sus have fled?

2 "Fear not, I am with thee, O be not dismayed,
For I am thy God, I will still give the aid;
I'll strengthen thee, help thee, and cause thee to stand
Upheld by my gracious, omnipotent hand.

3 "When through the deep waters I call thee to go,
The rivers of sorrow shall not overflow;
For I will be with thee thy trials to bless,
And sanctify to thee thy deepest distress.

4 "When through firey trials thy pathway shall lie,
My grace, all-sufficient, shall be thy supply,
The flame shall not hurt thee; I only design
Thy dross to consume, and thy gold to refine."
GEORGE KEITH.

THE CHRISTIAN'S HIDING PLACE. 8, 7.

Moderato. Mrs. A. E. GULICK.,

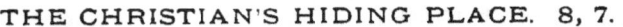

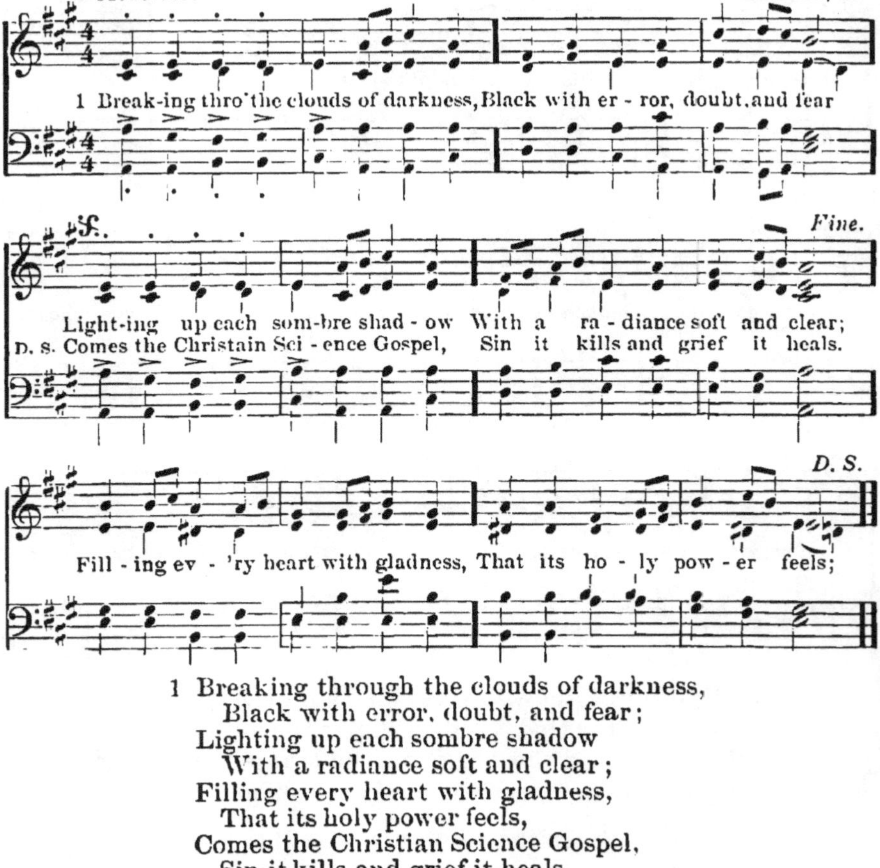

1 Breaking through the clouds of darkness,
Black with error, doubt, and fear;
Lighting up each sombre shadow
With a radiance soft and clear;
Filling every heart with gladness,
That its holy power feels,
Comes the Christian Science Gospel,
Sin it kills and grief it heals.

2 It will go across all oceans,
And be known in every land,
Till our sisters and our brothers,
All united in one band;
Raise to heaven their glad hosannas,
For a world from sin set free;
And to God, the Heavenly Father,
Then subdued will all things be.

F. L. HEYWOOD.

TRUTH.

SALOME. C. M.   LUDWIG VON BEETHOVEN.

1 City of God, how broad and far,
Out-spread Thy wall sublime;
The true, Thy chartered freeman are,
Of every age and clime.

1 City of God, how broad and far,
   Out-spread Thy wall sublime;
The true, Thy chartered freeman are,
   Of every age and clime.

2 One holy church, one army strong,
   One steadfast, high intent,
One working band, one harvest song,
   One King omnipotent.

3 How purely hath Thy speech come down
   From man's primeval youth;
How grandly hath Thine empire grown,
   Of Life, and Love, and Truth.

4 In vain the surge's angry shock,
   In vain the drifting sands:
Unharmed, upon the Eternal Rock,
   The Eternal City stands.
                SAMUEL JOHNSON.

TRUTH.

BONAR. P. M. — Dr. Bonar.

1 Know thou the Christ of God?
   His cross of Love?
Then art thou severed from this earth,
Linked to the city of thy birth,
   The land above.

2 Thy life is not below,
   'Tis all on high;
The Living One now lives for thee,
The Loving One now pleads for thee,
   Thou cans't not die.

3 Serve then the life of Faith,
   The life divine;
Live on in Him, the Living One,
Who holds thee with Him on His throne,
   His life is thine.

4 No rest, no slumber now;
   Watch and be strong;
Love is the smoother of the way,
And hope at midnight, as in day,
   Breaks out in song,

Dr. Bonar.

CHANT.

QUI HABITAT.   Unknown.

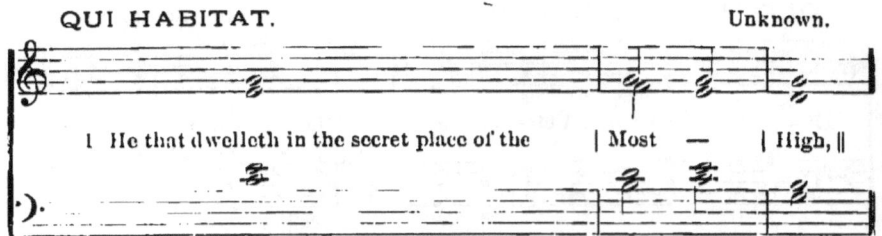

1 He that dwelleth in the secret place of the | Most— | High, ||
   shall abide under the | shadow of | the Al- | mighty.

2 I will say of the Lord, He is my refuge | and my | fortress, ||
   my God, in | Him— | will I | trust.

3 Because thou hast made the Lord, which | is my | refuge, ||
   even the Most | High, thy | habi- | tation.

4 There shall no evil be- | fall— | thee, || neither shall any |
   plague come | nigh thy | dwelling.

5 For He shall give His angels charge | over | thee, || to | keep
   thee in | all thy | ways.

6 They shall bear thee up | in their | hands, || lest thou dash
   thy | foot a- | gainst a | stone.

7 Thou shalt tread upon the | lion and | adder ; || the young
   lion and the dragon shalt thou | trample | under | feet.

Index of First Lines.

(Index of Tunes on 2d Page, Back of Title.)

First Line	Page
Abide with me! Fast falls the eventide	112
Abide not in the realms of dreams	161
Angels roll the Rock away	78
Around Bethesda's healing bower	122
Art thou weary	177
As shadows cast by cloud and sun	54
At the Lambs' high feast we sing	75
Beautiful thoughts, our angels bright	129
Beneath the shadow of the cross	188
Beneath the thick but breaking cloud	117
Between two seas we stand	196
Blest are the pure in heart	144
Breaking thro' the clouds of darkness	202
Bright was the guiding star that led	64
Calm on the list'ning ear of night	68
Calls out of darkness the voice of the	71
Children of the heavenly King	165
Christian! seek not yet repose	168
City of God, how broad and far	203
Come, O Thou universal Good	6
Come, Thou Almighty King	100
Come to the land of peace	154
Come unto Me, when shadows darkly	156
Come, ye disconsolate	192
Control my every thought	99
Day by day the manna fell	103
Everlasting arms of love	27
Every day hath toil and trouble	94
Fading, still fading, the last beam is	193
Faithful Shepherd, feed me	107
Father, hast Thou not a message	131
Father, in Thy most holy presence	26
Father of all, from land and sea	49
Father of all, in every age	28
Father most holy!	45
Fear not, O little flock	5
Fierce raged the tempest	158
Forbid them not, said the Master	136
Forever with the Lord	155
Give to the winds thy fears	7
Glorious things of Thee are spoken	189
Glory be to the Father	205
God of my life	19
God of the earth, the sky, the sea	33
God's glory is a wondrous thing	157
Go forth, ye heralds, in My name	113
Go forward, Christian soldier	132
Go, labor on, spend and be spent	119
Go to the pillow of disease	124
Gracious Spirit dwell with me	98
Green pastures and clear streams	186
Hail to the brightness of Zion's glad	135
Hail to the prince of life and peace	47
Harmonious Principle, ours evermore	23
Hark, my soul! it is the Lord	88
Hark, what celestial sounds	67
He always wins, who sides with God	11
Hear our prayer, O gracious Father	3
He is risen, He is risen	81
He leadeth me, O blessed thought	176
He liveth long, who liveth well	143
Help us, O Lord, Thy yoke to wear	110
He that dwelleth in the sacred place	206
Holy brethren, called and chosen	138
Holy Spirit, Source of gladness	171
Holy Spirit, Truth divine	13
How firm a foundation, ye saints	201
How happy is he born or taught	126
I cannot walk in darkness long	16
I heard the voice of Jesus say	182
I left the God of truth and light	172
Immortal Love, forever full	97
In heavenly love abiding	95
In some way or other	190
In Thee O Spirit true and tender	8
In the still air the music lies	146
I shall awake, however dread	141
Is this a day for me?	114
I thank Thee, O God	200
I trace your lines of arguement	24
Jesus, immortal King, arise	57
Jesus, Lord, we look to Thee	104
Jesus, Lover of my soul	58
Jesus, my Truth, my Way	59
Jesus shall reign where'er the sun	46
Jesus, Thou joy of loving hearts	51
Joy to the world, the Lord is come	62
Just as I am, without one plea	111
Know, my soul, thy full salvation	55
Know thou the Christ of God	204
Lead, kindly Light, amid the	31
Let there be light, thus spake the	179
Life of all that lives below	36
Light of life, seraphic fire	85
Light's glittering morn bedecks the	80
Lift your glad voices in triumph	77
Long ago in Holy Land	56
Lord of all being, throned afar	30

Index of First Lines.

First Line	Page
Love divine, all love excelling	93
Love is and was my Lord and King	90
Make channels for the streams of	92
Mercy, O thou Son of David	121
'Mid pleasures and palaces	147
Morning breaks upon the tomb	82
My country! 'tis of thee	167
My heart is full of whispered song	150
My Lord, how full of sweet content	42
My Shepherd's mighty aid	39
My soul with patience waits	175
Nearer, my God, to Thee	10
Now is the time approaching	187
Now when from matter I would turn	174
O come and dwell with me	102
Oh, backward looking, son of time	162
O he, whom Jesus, loved has truly	116
O fairest, born of Love and Light	89
O grant, dear Lord, this prayer	108
O Mother Love, Thou broodest still	91
O not in far off realms of space	20
Oh, sometimes gleams upon our sight	160
Oh, still in accents sweet and strong	181
O Tender One, O mighty One	120
O Thou eternal fount of love	22
O Thou in all Thy might so far	25
O Life that maketh all things new	198
O Life, we learn of Thee	4
O little town of Bethlehem	66
O Lord of heaven, and earth, and sea	18
O Love divine that stooped to share	84
O Love, O Life, our faith and sight	60
Open, Lord my inward ear	44
On the night of that last supper	69
Out of the distance and darkness so	195
Partners of a glorious hope	152
Peace be to this congregation	197
Praise God, from whom all blessings	205
Pray without ceasing, pray	169
Rejoice, the Lord is King	63
Rise crowned with light	194
Rock of Ages, cleft for me	125
See daylight is fading o'er earth and	32
See the ransomed millions stand	166
Shepherd, show us how to go	105
Sing them over again to me	148
Slowly o'er the sleeping world	191
Soldiers of Christ, arise,	153
Soldiers of the Cross, arise!	151
Sow in the morn thy seed	199
Still must I climb if I would rest	180
Still, still with Thee, when purple	137
Take up thy cross, the Savior said	53
Teach me my God and King	29
Teach me on Thee to wait	134
Teach us thy way, O God	109
Tell me not in mournful numbers	145
The day of resurrection	76
The harp at Nature's advent strung	163
The heavenly word proceeding forth	74
The Lord is my Shepherd, He makes	72
The Lord is my Shepherd, no want	37
The Lord is risen indeed	83
The morning kindles all the sky	79
The morning light is breaking	128
There is a land mine eye hath seen	142
There is one way, and only one	12
There's a wideness in God's mercy	87
The Spirit in our hearts	70
The starry firmament on high	140
The suffering child with an unerring	86
The thought I have my ample creed	12
The weary bird hath left the air	50
This God is the God we adore	21
This is the day of light	149
This world is poor from shore to	173
Tho' troubles assail and danger	9
Thou to Whom the sick and dying	118
Thou who art peace and unity	38
Thro' earth's vapors dimly seeing	185
Thy kingdom here	127
Thy power, O Lord! in days of old	123
Thy seamless robe conceals Thee not	48
Thy word, almighty Lord	40
"'Tis finished" so the Savior cried	52
To the haven of thy breast	61
To us a child of hope is born	65
Triumphant Zion, lift thy head	170
Walk in the light, so shalt thou know	139
Watchman tell us of the night	130
We bless Thee for Thy peace, O God	133
We giveThee, but Thine own	15
We pray no more, made lowly wise	35
We the weak ones, we the sinners	178
We wait in faith, in prayer we wait	159
What know we, Holy God, of Thee	43
What time the evening shadows fall	106
When gathering clouds around I	164
When I can read my title clear	184
When on the midnight of the east	73
When the blind suppliant in the way	115
When through the torn sail	101
When winds are raging o'er the	34
Who is thy neighbor	96
Word whose creative thrill	17
Ye know God but as Lord	183
Yes, we trust the day is breaking	41

www.ingramcontent.com/pod-product-compliance
Lightning Source LLC
Chambersburg PA
CBHW020903230426
43666CB00008B/1290